ANIMAL BEHAVIOR
INSTINCT, LEARNING, COOPERATION

Paolo Casale

Illustrations by: Gian Paolo Faleschini

BARRON'S

DoGi

English translation © Copyright 1999
by Barron's Educational Series, Inc.
Original edition © 1999 by Dogi spa, Florence, Italy
Title of original edition: *Il comportamento animale: instinto, apprendimento, cooperazione*

Italian edition by: Paolo Casale
Illustrations by: Gian Paolo Faleschini with the
collaboration of Leonardo Meschini
Editor: Francesco Milo
Graphic display: Sebastiano Ranchetti
Page make-up: Sebastiano Ranchetti

English translation by: Paula Boomsliter
for Lexis, Florence

All inquiries should be addressed to:
Barron's Educational Series, Inc.
250 Wireless Boulevard
Hauppauge, New York 11788
http://www.barronseduc.com

Library of Congress Catalog Card No. 99-64799

International Standard Book No. 0-7641-0952-9

Printed in Italy
9 8 7 6 5 4 3 2 1

Table of Contents

4   Ethology

16   The Two Extremes of Behavior

26   The Evolution of Behavior

36   To Everything There Is a Season . . .

44   Males and Females

56   Parents and Offspring

66   Prey and Predators

78   No Place Like Home

94   Social Behavior

108   Altruism

120   Index

ETHOLOGY

The behavior of animals is one of the most fascinating facets of nature. It is studied by a special branch of science called ethology. What exactly is animal behavior, how do we study it, and above all, why?

One of the characteristics that sets animals apart is their ability to move rapidly and efficiently in response to certain stimuli. This ability is determined by three important types of cells that are part of any organism: the sense cells that receive the stimulus, the nerve cells that transmit it, and the muscle cells that perform the movement. The sequences of actions that an animal performs in response to given stimuli depend on how these cells operate and are called *behaviors.*

This may seem strange, or overly simple, but before we decide, let's take a look at what happens at the biological level during a *behavioral response.*

Bats
Many bats are nocturnal animals that live by capturing insects as they fly. They do not need light to find their way; they emit sound waves as short cries, which are partly reflected by obstacles or prey. By analyzing the echos, bats can reconstruct their surrounding environment.

THE SENSES
How animals gather information from the environment determines their behavior, and varies from species to species.

First of all, the animal must be aware that a signal is coming in. In other words, a ray of light, a sound wave, or another type of stimulus must provoke an effect when it reaches the animal.

Recording these signals is the function of the sense cells, which are differentiated according to their specialization in receiving a certain type of signal—and only that type of signal. For example, the cells capable of receiving visual stimuli are insensitive to olfactory and auditory signals (smells and sounds). But the sense cells don't stop at receiving stimuli; another part of their job is to transform the stimuli into the electrical impulses that are the building blocks of the "language" used for transmitting information quickly

Zeroing in
(2) When there is a high concentration of molecules, the olfactory receptors signal the wing muscles to stop, and the fly "falls" near the food, which it reaches on foot.

"Sighting"
(1) The olfactory receptors of the fly record the presence of molecules emanating from food and direct the fly toward it.

The meal
(3) When the fly is on the source of food, the gustative receptors on the legs give a signal to stop and to extend the proboscis to eat.

The scorpion
The legs and rest of the body of the scorpion are equipped with receptors that sense the vibrations produced by the movement of the prey and indicate position and distance.

from one part of the body to another. We could compare this biological process to the electromechanical operation of a telephone; when we speak, the vibrations of our voice are transformed by the receiver into electrical signals that travel over the wire to the listener. In animals, the "wire" is replaced by the nerve cells, which send the message from the sensory organs to other nerve cells whose job it is to process the information. For this reason, these cells are grouped in larger or smaller bundles, according to need, and form that complex structure called the brain. But what do we mean when we say that the cells "process" information?

First phase
The ethologist observes an elephant ingesting dung and asks himself why the elephant is behaving this way.

The ethologist's hypotheses
(a) The dung is an alternative source of nourishment when normal forage is scarce.
(b) The dung supplies intestinal microorganisms that aid digestion.
(c) Eating dung is unusual behavior and derives from peculiarities in the individual under observation.

THE SCIENTIFIC METHOD
Theories are not formed by observation alone, but are rather the result of many phases of work from asking creative questions to checking possible answers.

An organism in imminent danger must counter with an immediate, precise response—with an action. Using other types of nerve cells as its messengers, the brain sends a command to the muscle cells. The effect of this command is to make the muscle cells contract. When the command is removed, the contraction ceases and the cells relax. When many muscle cells contract or relax at the same time, the whole muscle changes length and produces a movement.

By contracting different muscles, animals can perform such complex movements as swimming, flying, emitting sounds, or fighting.

Second phase

In order to single out the most plausible hypothesis, ethologists make further and more accurate observations. They note that other individuals also ingest dung and that all the individuals that do so are young.

Technology aids analysis

Under the microscope, we can see that the dung contains microorganisms capable of digesting cellulose, which is found in the elephants' normal food.

The ethologist's conclusions

The young elephants are eating the dung of the adults in order to procure the microorganisms they need to digest their food.

Chimpanzees are very similar to humans, but cannot speak. Some researchers have taught chimps to communicate using a keyboard, on which each key has a specific meaning; they have learned much about the chimps' ability to communicate in ways other than through human speech.

The three-spined stickleback is a fish, only a few inches long, that is found in Europe, Asia, and North America. In the spring, the males develop a characteristic red color on their undersides and fight among themselves for the breeding grounds. Cutouts of different forms and colors have been used to demonstrate that the aggressiveness of the males of this species is triggered by the red coloration of the abdomen.

IN THE LABORATORY It is sometimes useful, when studying the mechanisms of behavior, to observe animals in conditions that permit controlling the stimuli they receive.

Certain actions give rise to what is called "behavior." A specific behavior will generally be the most suitable action for reacting to the situation in which the animal finds itself.

Obviously, the more complex the nervous system, the more elaborate may be the response to the stimulus—the behavior. One of the reasons for this is that a complex nervous system can memorize information for future use.

Ethology, the science that studies the behavior of animals, directs most of its attention to complex behaviors, since their causes and development are often hard to understand.

There are two ways to study a behavior: One consists of analyzing

Sea turtles

As soon as they are hatched, the tiny turtles leave the beach and head for the open sea. Only the females ever return to land; they come back to the same beach, many years later, to lay their eggs. In order to understand whether or not the turtles use the earth's magnetic field to find their way, some individuals were placed in special tanks in which the direction of the magnetic field could be varied. It was found that the little turtles swam in different directions as the magnetic field was changed.

the "mechanism" by which the animal under observation reacts to a given stimulus; the other tries to understand why, over the course of its evolution, a certain species has developed a certain behavior—in what way a certain kind of behavior gives the animal an advantage. This is what the *ethologists* are most interested in learning when they study animal behavior.

How do we study behavior?

The first phase of research consists of observing one or more animals. These preliminary observations allow ethologists to formulate new questions, such as "Why do these animals behave as they do?" or "Why does this species behave differently from other species?" The ethologists then formulate a series of possible answers. How

THE ETHOLOGIST'S TOOLS
An important skill for a researcher is applying technology that was developed in other fields, or inventing completely new technologies.

Marking
Using tags, each a different color or with a different code, ethologists can distinguish various individuals in a population and follow their activities over one or more years.

AN ACCURATE DESCRIPTION
is the first step in understanding a behavior, but sometimes it is difficult to observe single individuals. Some species of bee eaters, for example, nest in colonies and dig their nests into steep slopes in the Mediterranean region. Many questions have been asked about the interactions between the members of the colony and their migrations to Africa, where they spend the winter.

do they know which is correct?

One good way of proceeding is to consider the plausible answers as *hypotheses* and to formulate *predictions* based on them.

Let's suppose we have observed birds engaged in what looks like danc-ing. If we hypothesize that the dance is a courting ritual, our prediction might be that all the individuals performing the dance are males, that they behave in this manner during the mating season, and that they dance only in the presence of a female of the species. Or our hypothesis could be that the dance is a danger signal, and in this case our prediction might be that it is performed by both males and females and only when a potential predator approaches. After having formulated as many hypotheses and relative predictions as come to mind, ethologists again observe the animals to learn if what they see conforms to their predictions. Sometimes, no prediction is borne out by observation, in which case new hypotheses are needed.

In any case, even when ethologists have communicated their conclusions to other researchers, there is no guarantee that they will be accepted by everyone,

Pairing
Do these birds form new pairs each year or does a pair remain together for more than one reproductive season? Do the birds mate outside of the pair?

Caring for the young
Who brings food to the young? Only the parents, or other individuals as well?

The females
Do the females return to the same spot each year to nest?

and it is always possible that further observation will demonstrate that the conclusions are wrong. In this case, there is nothing to do but to start over.

This procedure is used in all fields of science. Advancing theories that may later be proved wrong is not actually "wrong"; the only truly incorrect approach is to refuse to question even the most widely accepted theories.

Animal behavior and human behavior

Why do we study behavior? Curiosity is one of the most important human attributes; what's more, our species, like all the others, is part of an ecosys-

THE FIRST ETHOLOGISTS
All animals "study" one another in order to survive. Thanks to their intellect, humans have developed this capacity to a greater extent than other animals.

Hunters' lore
Hunters memorize the movements of game and tell other hunters about them; thus, humans can predict the behavior of the hunted animals and take them by surprise.

tem and has always interacted with other animals. Some of these are dangerous predators; others are useful sources of food. For this reason, understanding the various species and therefore being able to predict their behavior has always been extremely important.

The study of the biological bases of animal behavior, however, originated fairly recently, with the pioneering work of such researchers as Konrad Lorenz, Niko Tinbergen, and Karl von Frisch, who were awarded the Nobel Prize in 1972.

Lorenz began his research in the belief that discoveries relating to animals could help in understanding human behavior, which, although we

Experience
Humans are also well aware of the behavior of those animals that would try to hunt them; they know they must be careful near the water where a crocodile might be lying in wait.

take it for granted, is extremely complex. Both the complexity of a person's behavior and the fact that it is taken for granted depend on the person's having received, during his or her life, a wealth of ideas composed of language, mime, interacting with other persons, a conception of himself or herself and of the universe, certain values, and so on. All this knowledge, which will vary according to the social context in which one is brought up and educated, shapes the way an individual acts. Thus, in our species, more than in any other, behavior varies greatly among different populations and among single individuals.

Examining the similarities and the differences among the behaviors of different populations can help us understand how they developed from common patterns in response to different environmental, social, and economic factors. In the same way, comparing human behaviors with those of other species can help us to understand why we have developed certain behavioral characteristics instead of others, and in what way these behaviors provided advantages that permitted our ancestors to evolve into modern human beings.

Finally, it is interesting to analyze how useful these behavioral patterns, or models for response to external stimuli, are in today's world, which has been radically transformed, with respect to the world of primitive human beings, by human beings themselves.

HUMAN ETHOLOGY
Using ethological methods to study human behavior can reveal a great deal about its importance in evolution.

Social interaction
Why do two people shake hands when they meet? In a social species like ours, individuals must be on good terms with one another. One way is to make friendly gestures.

Competitive sports
Why do humans engage in sports contests? The members of a social group are always competing among themselves and with other groups. Sports probably help humans to express this tendency to compete, common to all animals, in a harmless manner.

Pairing
Why do people form couples, and why is physical contact important between the partners? The fundamental unit of human society is made up of a man and a woman, who must create a strong, lasting relationship in order to care for their children. This behavior is typical of our species.

THE TWO EXTREMES OF BEHAVIOR

Certain behaviors are *instinctive* as compared to all other types, which are instead formed by the individual's experience. What are instincts? It is correct to so clearly distinguish between types of behavior?

As we have seen, a behavior is the result of the nervous system's processing of signals that come from the sensory organs. Thus, if two animals behave differently, it means they have either received different stimuli or performed different processing.

The latter case is a possibility because processing depends on the characteristics of the nervous system, some of which are unchanged since birth; others are acquired through experience and therefore vary according to the type of stimuli the animal has

Zebras
react by fleeing. Given their physical structure, this is the most effective behavior to avoid being caught.

Facing a predator
Both elephants and zebras consider the lion a threat, but react in very different ways.

received during its life. A behavior that relies on past experience is *acquired* or *learned*; otherwise, it is *innate* or *inborn*.

Is it correct to say that an inborn behavior—a behavior that is already present at birth—is inherited from the parents, and that learned behavior depends on the environment alone? Not quite. First of all, to be able to use their experience, animals need an adequate nervous system. For example, some birds, such as jays, can accurately memorize the places where they store their winter supplies. They have this ability because their nervous system is structured in such a way that the memorization centers are particularly sensitive to visual stimuli. Wolves, on the other hand, recognize the other members of their pack by their smell, and have memorization centers that are particularly sensitive to olfactory stimuli. The basic characteristics of the nervous system, such as sensitivity to visual or olfactory stimuli, are inherited. They permit the acquiring of experience, which comes from the environment. According to its predisposition,

DIFFERENT BEHAVIORS
Behavior varies from one species to the next, just as physical attributes do. Comparing behaviors helps us understand how each can be useful.

Elephants
are large and armed with strong tusks, and can therefore stand up to a predator. It is usually the task of the lead female to intimidate a lion.

which is hereditary, and its being influenced by experience, which is environmental, the nervous system will have a greater or lesser capacity for learning.

From what we have seen thus far it is clear that all behaviors depend on the nervous system and its characteristics. The nervous system develops as a result of information contained in the organism's DNA, genetic information transmitted by the parents to their offspring, which contains all the instructions for the development and operation of the cells that make up the body. Thus, the basic characteristics of the nervous system are controlled by heredity. But behaviors often have an environmental component, however small. Think of identical twins: Each received identical genetic information, but twins develop different tastes and behaviors according to the different stimuli each receives.

The best way of meeting needs

All species have innate behaviors and forms, however simple, of learned behavior. Why isn't all behavior based on learning,

A complex inheritance
Although the movements made by a spider when it captures and wraps it prey in its silk thread are very complex, they are not the result of experience but, rather, are inborn. The spider's nervous system is too simple to permit learning such a technique.

Rats exploit every possible source of food and will taste anything that seems edible. The rat has developed the capacity to associate the sensation of nausea with foods that have been shown to be poisonous, but cannot associate pains of external origin with flavors, because these conditions are not linked in nature. The rat's capacity for learning is limited.

The *chlamydosaurus*, or frilled dragon, is an Australian reptile that defends itself from predators by opening a fold of skin on its neck to appear larger than it actually is. This is a simple reaction, and thus it may be more convenient for it to be considered innate rather than learned.

THE USEFULNESS OF LEARNING
Not all animals manifest behaviors that can be modulated by experience, because this type of behavior depends on the needs and the intellectual capacities of each species.

The woodpecker finch, native to the Galapagos islands, lives on insect larvae it extracts from the trunks of trees. The innate tendency of this species to manipulate thorns and twigs, perfected through experience, permits it to capture its prey even when it cannot reach it with its beak alone.

Involution
The male of the deep-sea angler is much smaller than the female, to which it adheres to receive the nutrients it needs. Because of this parasitic life, the behavior of the animal, like its body, is extremely simple.

SIMPLE AND COMPLEX BEHAVIOR

The complexity of behavior is not determined by the actions of the nervous system alone, but also by the needs of the species.

Hunters

Certain starfish prey on bivalves such as oysters. In order to eat, the starfish must first locate its prey, then open the shell far enough to insert its stomach, which can turn inside out like a glove. The gastric juices digest the meat of the bivalve, transforming it into a nutrient liquid that is then "imbibed" by the starfish.

Filter feeders
The peacock worm is a marine annelid that lives in a tube it builds using grains of sand and mucus. It feeds on particles in suspension in the water, which are intercepted by its crown of tentacles and descend to the mouth. Animals that lead a sedentary life have no need to develop complex behavior.

which to us humans may seem the best way of doing things?

The capacity to learn is very useful in those cases in which it is impossible to foresee what type of behavior might be needed in a given situation. For example, the fox lives in the most varied environments and can live on many different kinds of prey: fish, insects, birds, small mammals. For a fox, it is useful to learn what type of prey can be found in its territory and how to hunt it, since these are factors that can change with time and can be different in different territories.

But learning means memorizing information and processing it. To be able to do this, the animal needs time to acquire experience—to gather information—and a great deal of energy in order to build and support a brain capable of performing these functions. Consequently, the learning strategy is not always the most advantageous. For example, it would be pointless for a nocturnal animal, such as the owl, which is not physically adapted to daytime activity, to have to waste time and energy learning to hunt at night and sleep during the day. It is much safer and more efficient for this type of behavior to be innate.

Imprinting

There is a moment in the life of every animal, that of its birth, when there can be no learned behavior. But as soon as it is born, every individual must be able to perform simple actions, such

Birdsong

Generally, male birds learn the song of their species by listening to a parent, even though the basic melodic structure is innate. The male cuckoo must vocalize like its own species, not that of other birds in whose nest the female cuckoo may lay eggs; thus, the young cuckoos do not retain auditory imprinting.

IMPRINTING

Some species need to acquire information quickly and accurately. This mode of memorization, called imprinting, takes place early in life but in different periods according to the species and the type of information to be acquired.

as eating, in order to survive. For example, a newborn colt must be able to move with the herd as the adults range in search of food and water. This type of behavior is, by definition, inborn. In other cases it may be extremely important that newborns be able to use the first information gathered from the outside world.

A classical example of this special type of learning is *imprinting*—the ability to memorize a certain type of information only during a certain period. To understand its usefulness, think of a newborn animal that must be able to follow its mother in order to survive.

The ability to move independently and to follow another individual may

Olfactive imprinting
It is important that the young of some species of shrews never lose track of their mother, since they are completely dependent on her. They therefore learn very early to recognize her odor, so that they are able to follow her anywhere.

Environmental imprinting
The cuckoo lays its eggs in the nests of other birds. Each female produces only one type of egg, which is identical to that form which she hatched and also very similar to the eggs of one or few host species. Were she to choose the wrong nest, her egg would be easily recognized and eliminated. It has been suggested that the female memorizes, by imprinting, the type of environment in which she was raised and finds an analogous setting for her eggs, thus increasing her chances of selecting the nest of the correct adoptive species.

be inborn behavior, but recognizing one's mother in a group is not. It is therefore useful that the newborn learn to rapidly and accurately distinguish its mother's features—her look, her smell, and her voice.

Inborn and learned behaviors in humans

Humans, with only a few innate behaviors, are the animals that more than any other make use of the results of learning.

This "learning strategy" probably evolved to make humans capable of handling many different types of situations. Our species does not rely solely on physical characteristics for its survival; humans are not always able to fight off the attack of a predator, or able to escape it, nor are we as individuals capable of capturing and killing any except the smallest prey. In all these activities, we make use of tools that can be built and used only thanks to our great capacity for learning.

Likewise, we humans combat bad weather by building shelters and procuring warm clothing that permit us to live from the equator to the poles.

Another element that is fundamental for our survival is efficient cooperation among individuals, which is impossible without an elaborate system of communications. The price we pay for all these skills is a long childhood and an extended period of parental care, during which we accumulate much of the information we will need during our adult life.

Bunched fingers
For an Italian, this gesture means "What do you want?" but for a Turk it means "Good!" and for a Yemenite, "Wait!"

Yawning
is a coordinated set of movements that no one needs to learn. At the same time, it is a stimulus to the observer to yawn in turn. Various hypotheses have been proposed to explain the usefulness of yawning. It may help to relax the head muscles, but in some social species it could also have the function of synchronizing group activities such as rest.

Smiling
is common to all human beings and constitutes a sign of friendliness that is visible from afar. It is so important for the social life of our species that it is inborn behavior. Smiling begins early in infancy, even in blind people who have not been able to see and imitate the expression.

THE EVOLUTION OF BEHAVIOR

The animal world offers an incredible variety of physical forms and typical behaviors. Harmony among an animal's form, its behavior, and the environment in which it lives is the result of evolution. But how does a behavior evolve?

The more we learn about animals' lives and the environments in which they live, the more their characteristics, which at first might seem bizarre, appear to be essential. Behavior, which together with physical structure makes an animal perfectly efficient, is no exception.

As we observe this harmony among physical and behavioral characteristics, we might ask what came first, the egg that must be incubated in order to hatch, or the brooding hen; in other words, do physical characteristics determine the evolution of a

BODY AND BEHAVIOR
Behavior and physical structure cannot evolve independently, since each must be appropriate for the other.

The freshwater turtle
has a lighter shell than that of the tortoise. This makes it more agile in the aquatic environment, where it seeks shelter when threatened by predators on land.

The origin of shells and carapaces
is still a mystery, but they certainly developed in animals similar to today's lizards in environmental and behavioral conditions that made such protection more of a benefit than a hindrance. Later, as conditions changed, it became useful to strengthen the armor and use immobility as a defense strategy.

behavior, or the opposite? The answer is "Probably both."

We must remember that evolution rarely proceeds by leaps and bounds, because major changes would upset the functioning of an organism. For example, a pigeon attempting to dig its nest into a tree trunk, as the woodpecker does, without the same kind of beak, muscles, and bone structure, could not succeed and would probably hurt itself. It is also improbable that all the characteristics of a woodpecker would appear suddenly in the offspring of a pigeon.

The key to evolution of new adaptations to environmental conditions is

The tortoise cannot evolve fleeing as an avoidance behavior, since its heavy, stiff shell makes it too slow and clumsy. Hiding in its shell is therefore the animal's only hope of saving itself.

The lizard cannot evolve an avoidance behavior of immobility, except among certain species, since its body is very vulnerable. It seeks safety by fleeing, although some species are slow runners but well protected by spines and cryptic coloration.

instead versatility, that is, the possibility for a characteristic to perform more than one function. For example, a small change may make a structure such as a beak or teeth suitable for handling a type of food different from an animal's normal fare. A few generations later, the animal's descendants will try and be able to eat that other food when their principal nourishment is scarce, thus encouraging the development of a new behavior. Likewise, a habitual behavior, such as fleeing from a predator, may change. For example, a rabbit escapes predators by hiding in bushes or in its burrow; if a new behavior, such as climbing a tree, should meet with success, any later improvement in the strength of the limbs or the force of the claws will permit the animal to climb other types of trees and to climb higher.

What does this mean? Simply that structure and behavior must both change if some time later the animal is to possess characteristics that are completely different from the originals.

The evolution of behavior

A behavior is simply one of the great number of characteristics that permit an individual to survive and reproduce in its environment, and as with the others, it is subject to natural selection. Just what is natural selection, and how does it work?

Natural selection is a process that permits animals to develop characteristics that are advantageous in the environment in which they live. The process usually works on genetically

THE ORIGIN OF THE WHALES
The evolution of the behavior and the physical structure of the cetaceans is a good example of how these two factors influence each other. Between 55 and 60 million years ago, the drift of India toward continental Asia caused the formation of a closed sea rich in food, a whole new array of nutritional opportunities begging to be exploited.

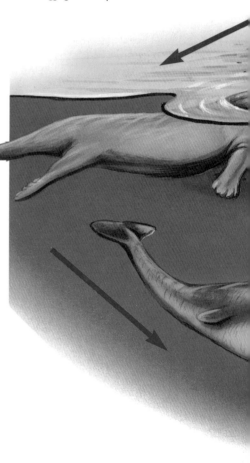

The mesonychids
It is probable that the ancestors of the whales were members of a group of terrestrial carnivores, called mesonychids. They altered their feeding behavior when many new marine species became potential prey, and thus took the first step in an extraordinary transformation.

The new environment
in which the prey was captured produced intense selection that allowed the descendants of the mesonychids to develop anatomical characteristics suitable for moving more easily in the water.

Modern cetaceans
Whales and dolphins no longer have any contact with dry land, and their bodies are perfectly adapted to life in the seas. Likewise, all their behavior, not only feeding, has changed to fit the marine environment.

The wolf
is a predator that lives in groups called packs. The members of the pack cooperate when they hunt.

USEFUL CHARACTERISTICS
By mating generation after generation of wolves with characteristics useful for humans, we have produced today's breeds of dogs, animals whose behavior is very different from that of their wild ancestors. For example, the Abruzzi shepherd dog has lost the hunting instinct that is typical of wolves and even other breeds of dogs, and is thus harmless to the flock.

Defending the flock
The Abruzzi shepherd dog defends its flock from intruders, just as wolves defend their territories, for which the flock may be said to represent a substitute.

ARTIFICIAL SELECTION
The selection process used by humans to produce domestic animals is a fast, simplified version of natural selection.

transmitted characteristics, that is, those inherited by the offspring from their parents. The rare events that give rise to more or less significant changes are called *mutations,* basic alterations in hereditary material.

What's more, in those species in which sexual reproduction takes place—when a male and female mate to produce offspring—the genetic characteristics are reshuffled with every generation in such a way that the gene combinations of the offspring are different from those of the parents. For example, if one of the parents has long red fur and the other has short black fur, some of the offspring may well be born with long black fur. Occasional mutations of the DNA, and above all the commixing of the parents' genes, generate a great diversity among individuals, some of which will have gene combinations and types that offer more advantages than others. Due to limited resources such as food, shelter, or mates, not all the individuals that are born survive.

Among those that survive, not all succeed in reproducing, and among those that reproduce, not all have the same number of offspring during their lives.

All things considered, it is probable that those individuals that succeed in generating the greatest number of descendants will be those that by chance inherited the gene combinations that produce the characteristics most suitable for living in the environment in which they live. And since the genes they inherited are those their offspring will in turn inherit, later generations will possess fewer of the inefficient gene combinations and more of the efficient ones. This is what we mean by "selection."

Generation after generation, this process can bring about great alterations, and it will operate faster when environmental changes occur.

Environmental conditions are the "judges" of selection, and to stay "in the running," a population must continually improve its performance.

Cultural transmission

There are also behaviors that are inherited culturally, not genetically. This is possible only in the case of animals that have inherited (genetically) a complex nervous system that makes them good learners. If an individual, through its personal experience, invents a certain behavior that leads to an advantage, such as obtaining more food, its offspring and the other members of its group may be able to learn the new behavior by imitating its inventor,

THE CULTURAL SPECIES

The macaques of Japan have a well-developed capacity to transmit learned experiences. This was demonstrated in the 1950s, when biologists began supplying grain and potatoes to a troop of macaques as they observed the development and spread of new traditions.

The innovators

The younger individuals are more likely to explore and are the main inventors of the troop. Imo invented potato washing when she was two and the grain separation technique at four. The second technique, which is more complex from the conceptual point of view, required greater experience.

A genius

A female named Imo modified the normal behavior regarding cleaning food by dunking the potatoes in water to better free them of dirt. The monkeys picked up the grains of wheat from the sand one by one until Imo invented another technique— throwing handfuls of dirty wheat into the sea and collecting the grains, which floated while the sand sank.

The conservatives
The older individuals, especially the males, tend to explore less and be more conservative.

Only rarely do individuals older than 7 to 10 years adopt new techniques invented and used by the younger monkeys.

instead of having to invent it themselves. If many individuals do this, it is probable that new improvements will come about more and more rapidly.

In humans, more than in any other animal, behavior has evolved in this way. Thanks to our intelligence, to our long childhood learning period, and to language, we have discovered and invented many things and have efficiently transmitted them to later generations. In order to understand the importance of cultural transmission in our evolutionary history, let's compare the ability of humans to transmit experiences with the rate of technological development.

In the beginning, when language was spoken and not written, history and culture were limited by how much a person could remember. The invention of writing permitted humans to accumulate and transmit great quantities of knowledge. Since our capacity to discover or to invent depends on how much information and technology is already available, writing caused culture to grow exponentially, especially after it was teamed with efficient methods of distribution—first printing, and today the information networks. The resulting technological development has favored the increase of the human population, but this fact has been catastrophic for entire ecosystems and threatens to jeopardize our very survival. We can only hope that cultural development will succeed, before it is too late, in providing solutions to the planetary problems that advances and development are creating.

THE EFFECT OF INFORMATION
The human species is unique in its great variety of social structures and individual activities. These all depend on the type of information, or culture, received by individuals.

Communication
is a foundation of cooperation among humans. The more complex the cooperation, the more efficient must be the communication, since frequent exchanges of messages are needed to coordinate the actions of different people.

TRIBAL CULTURE

The culture of the members of a tribe, or group of people, is generally made up of information about only the limited environment in which the tribe lives. But the members of the tribe have knowledge about their world that extends to every detail.

CONTACTS

In ancient times, it was rare for a tribe to be on good terms with more than one of the neighboring tribes. It was therefore difficult to receive information about far-off places and peoples, and each isolated tribe developed its own language and traditions.

TECHNOLOGICAL CULTURE

Explorers exploit the information gathered by other people, either in the past or present. However, they often know nothing about how what they use operates, just as they may know nothing about certain natural features of their own environment.

TO EVERYTHING THERE IS A SEASON...

Different types of behavior are not used haphazardly or all at once; each must be expressed in the situation in which it is useful, and in no other. How do animals know when the time is right?

The many behaviors that an individual may express are the result of lengthy evolution. This means that they are indispensable for the animal, and the animal would not be suitable for its environment without them. Just think of a hen that stops incubating its eggs; it would be unable to reproduce. Likewise, expressing a behavior in a situation in which it is not called for can be a great waste of energy, of time, and of occasions to obtain other advantages, not to mention that it could place the animal in serious danger. For example,

ALTERNATIVE BEHAVIORS
In what appear to be similar circumstances, the same animal may react differently if secondary factors vary. This is why the reactions of animals are so difficult to predict.

if a mouse flees for no good reason, it expends a lot of energy that it cannot recover because it no longer has enough time to eat correctly. Nor will it be able to reproduce; the more it runs, the more it risks being located by a predator or even running right out to meet it.

In order to be able to do the right thing at the right time, animals have developed certain mechanisms that are activated by specific stimuli. A sudden noise or movement will generally trigger a fear reaction, causing the animal to run or defend itself. The scent or sight of food provokes feeding behavior; the presence of a partner, courting; and so on. But that's not quite all there is to it. For example, if the presence of

The lone wolf
The wolf will not attack a group of caribou without the help of other wolves, since it would be a waste of time and energy for the wolf to try to capture such a large prey alone.

The bull elephant shows no interest in a group of females not far away. Since the females are not in estrus—they are not ready for mating—any attempt at courtship would be a waste of time and effort for the male.

a possible partner were all that was needed to stimulate a bird to initiate courtship, it might do so outside of the season most favorable to reproduction, causing useless wastes of time and energy. This does not usually happen, because behaviors are not spurred by a single stimulus, but rather by an often very complex set of circumstances that predispose the animal to reacting positively when the key stimulus—what actually triggers the behavioral response—presents itself. Such factors as the sexual maturity of the individual, the temperature, the photoperiod (the number of hours of daylight), and others, "tell" the animal whether it is ready to reproduce and when the time is right to do so. As in a missile launch, the animal will be ready to reproduce only if all systems are "go." The actual launch, however, takes place only when the ignition button is pushed; in our case, when the animal meets a potential partner.

THE SEASONAL CYCLES
Animals perceive the changes in the seasons and exhibit the most suitable behavior for each period of the year.

The role of hormones

The mechanisms underlying these processes are complex, for the simple reason that they must take into account a great deal of information of many different origins. Often the hormones, substances released into the blood that tell all the organs on which the success of the behavior will depend to "get ready," are involved. Hormones are produced by special glands in response to various signals originating both within the organism and outside of it. The nerve cells are influenced both by the signals transmitted by

Reproduction

White storks reproduce over much of Europe during the spring, when they can find sufficient food to feed their young.

Migration

In the fall, storks from eastern Europe migrate to Africa, flying over the Bosphorus. The following spring they make the return journey to their breeding grounds.

Wintering

The winter is spent on the African continent, in regions south of the Sahara.

other nerve cells and by the hormones, in such a way as to produce a given behavior only when a specific combination of these two types of signals is received. For example, the sex hormones are present in high concentrations only in individuals that have reached sexual maturity and only during the reproductive season. Then and only then will an animal be ready to initiate courtship when it encounters a member of the opposite sex. In other circumstances, instead, the stimuli involved are less specific, and it is difficult to pick out the key one—if there is one at all. This is the case with winter hibernation or migration; the hedgehog, for example, starts looking for a den for the winter as its internal compulsion to do so becomes stronger and stronger. It is impossible to say

POPULATION DENSITY
One of the most important parameters that can change behavior, especially in the social species, is the number of individuals forced to live together in a single environment.

Overcrowding
When density is very high there is greater competition for resources, including a good spot on the waterfront and access to the females. In a situation like this, it is more probable that depending on the species, the males will engage in vicious fights.

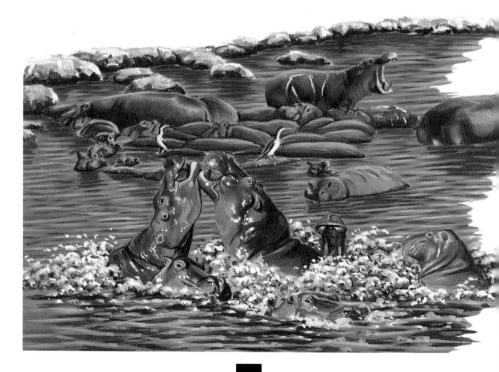

Space for everyone
At low population densities, violent fights among adult hippopotami are rare events.

exactly when the animal will perform the action, because it does not depend on a momentary signal transmitted rapidly by the nerve cells but rather on hormone levels, that is, the concentrations of certain substances in the body. These in turn are determined by generalized stimuli and act over longer time periods.

Humans' cycles

Humans are not commanded by seasonal cycles such as hibernation or migration, although studies have shown that levels of many hormones in humans fluctuate by season. These adaptations are typical of animals that live in climates where the difference between summer and winter temperatures is considerable. In our probable place of origin, tropical Africa, the differences between the seasons are not great enough to warrant these types of behavior.

Neither does human reproduction depend on specific periods, unless we count the woman's ovulation cycle. Consequently, in man, courting and mating can take place at any time. It is believed that this adaptation helps create a stable relationship between a man and a woman, different from other species in which the male and female stay together for only short periods, and it helps guarantee the long periods of parental care that human children require.

The human organism is, however, governed by other rhythms that come from an internal clock set to day and night. These are called *circadian rhythms*. Anyone who has taken a long plane trip will have suffered from jet lag, that uncomfortable period when the internal clock is still set to the time zone the traveler started from.

In the big cities
The population densities of modern societies are far beyond those for which our evolution has prepared us. This has led to alterations of the original social behaviors. The fact that it is impossible to establish contacts with everyone else creates indifference toward others, who are often considered almost a part of the scenery.

The origins of societies
The tribe is the original social condition. In the tribe, each individual interacts with all the others and reciprocal help and cooperation are the order of the day.

MALES AND FEMALES

Natural selection, and life itself, would be impossible without reproduction. Directly or indirectly, all the other characteristics of an organism, including behavior, revolve around reproduction.

There exist many reproduction strategies, but all fall into a few basic categories. First of all, reproduction may be sexual or asexual. In the first case, two individuals mingle their genes to create new combinations; in the second, a single individual generates identical copies of itself. The planarian, a flatworm, is a good example—if one is cut in two, each part will reconstruct a complete organism. The advantage of sexual reproduction is that the offspring are not identical to either of the parents, each having a

Elephant seals
In the spring, the males fight violently among themselves for control of the areas occupied by the females. This behavior probably evolved because the females unite in groups to give birth and raise their young.

The females are ready to mate again right after giving birth, and will mate with the male that controls the area.

Control is therefore equal to an extraordinary reproductive opportunity.

different combination of the characteristics of both.

In this way, it is more probable that at least one of the young will possess features suitable for surviving in changed environmental conditions.

In some species that practice sexual reproduction, there are male individuals and female individuals, while in other species the same individual may perform the role of either male or female, either at the same time or at different times during the course of its life.

The species in which the individuals are of only one sex, in at least one phase of their lives, are the most interesting from the ethological point of view,

SEXUAL REPRODUCTION
Animals recombine their genetic information in different ways to give rise to new individuals.

Snails
are hermaphrodites, that is, each individual is both male and female. During mating, each supplies sperm to fertilize its partner's eggs. In this case, there are no differences in the behaviors of the two members of the pair, since their relationship is perfectly symmetrical.

Labroides dimidiatus
A school of *Labroides dimidiatus*—a species of Pacific cleaner fish—is composed of one male and many females. But sex is not firmly established at birth; all the individuals are born female. If the male of the school dies, one of the largest females changes sex and takes his place.

COMPETING TO BE CHOSEN
The females of the kob antelopes
mate with the strongest males,
whom they recognize on the basis
of the area each male seizes and
defends from the other males.

The strongest males
have succeeded in
taking over the
small central areas
of the arena.

 since individuals of opposite sexes assume different, specific roles and consequently develop specific behaviors.

There are three major modes of interaction between the two sexes. In *polygamy* a male mates with more than one female; in *polyandry* the female mates with more than one male; in *monogamy* a single female and a single male mate.

Why do all these possibilities exist? In order to answer this question we must analyze the investments made by the two sexes in reproduction, that is, how much energy each must expend to obtain offspring. The fundamental difference depends on the size of the

46

The males on the outskirts of the arena have larger territories but less probability of mating with the females.

The females choose the males at the center of the arena for their mates.

gametes, the cells—one from the mother, one from the father—that unite to create the first cell of the new organism. While females produce large gametes (eggs), the males produce tiny ones (sperm). It may seem strange that we distinguish between the sexes on the basis of this feature, when there exist so many other, more conspicuous differences, but the differences in the forms and behavior of males and females basically all depend on the size and the contents of the gametes each produces. The females spend a great deal of time and energy to produce their eggs, which contain all the material needed for the development of the new individual.

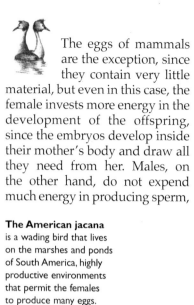

The eggs of mammals are the exception, since they contain very little material, but even in this case, the female invests more energy in the development of the offspring, since the embryos develop inside their mother's body and draw all they need from her. Males, on the other hand, do not expend much energy in producing sperm, which contain no nutrients but only the genetic information needed for building the new organism. For these reasons, males can produce many more gametes much more quickly than

The American jacana
is a wading bird that lives on the marshes and ponds of South America, highly productive environments that permit the females to produce many eggs. The nests are rather precarious and the birds risk losing their eggs in the water.

The limpkin
lives in the same environment as the jacana but has evolved a different relationship between the sexes; male and female stay together and cooperate in caring for and raising their offspring.

A UNIQUE STRATEGY
The best strategy for a female jacana is to lay more than one clutch of eggs and to entrust each to a different male, rather than dedicating her full energy to a single nest. The males are thus a precious resource for the females, who compete to include as many males as possible in their territories. The roles of the sexes are practically the opposite of the typical pattern.

Different roles
While the female invests energy in producing eggs, the males of the jacana invest energy in incubating the eggs. If the brood is lost, they are ready to mate again at any time. If the male did not cooperate, the effort involved in laying and caring for the eggs would be excessive for the female and would jeopardize her chances for reproduction.

The male makes himself useful
If the female is not able to provide for the brood by herself, the male may put more energy into helping his partner in caring for the young.

can females. It follows that while the number of offspring a female can bear during the course of her life will depend only on her own biological and behavioral characteristics, the number of offspring that can be had by a male is potentially limited only by the number of times it mates, and is therefore much higher.

As a result of these differences, the female has much more to lose in a less-than-optimal mating than does the male. The female thus tends to be more selective, that is, more careful to choose the male with the best characteristics in order to guarantee that her offspring will have the features most suitable for the environment in which they will live. The male can be less selective and place more emphasis on the quantity of his matings than on the quality of his partner, that is, more on sheer numbers than on the characteristics of the offspring.

Since females are selective, males are forced to compete to be chosen. As a result of this female prerogative, the strongest males will monopolize great numbers of females. We therefore have polygamy—the males have the advantage of producing many offspring, and the females can be fertilized by the best males.

However, if the survival of the offspring requires more energy than the female alone can provide, it is in the male's interest to cooperate in raising the young. In this case, the males cannot expend time and energy in courting many females. Each male mates with only one female and then dedicates his energies to caring for the offspring. A monogamous situation has thus been created.

In very special circumstances, the reproductive investment of the males is greater than that of the females. In these cases, we would expect the males to be selective toward the females and the females to compete to mate—and this is exactly what happens in the polyandrous species.

Sexual selection and courting

To sum up, differences in investments for reproduction have produced different strategies and therefore different behavior in the two sexes. But where does *sexual dimorphism*, or the physical diversities between males and females, come from? This is one of the most fascinating examples of how

The great crested grebe lives in temperate zones in Europe and Australia. It is monogamous; male and female form a permanent couple and care for their young.

COURTSHIP BEHAVIOR

Using the behavioral capacities of their species, males and females have developed complex rituals for choosing each other.

Advertising

During courting, the colored tufts around the head, a characteristic of this grebe, are held erect. Male and female do not have specific behaviors; each performs the same complex ritual.

The "dance of the grasses"

This is a phase of courtship in which the two birds collect fragments of vegetation and move their heads from side to side. It is thought that this ritual incorporates aspects of nest-building behavior that uses aquatic plants.

SEXUAL SELECTION
Competition for mating leads males and females to evolve sex-specific features.

The reedbuck lives in the Indian savannahs. The males fight to mate with the females. Like many other species of herbivorous mammals, the males possess large, powerful horns that they use during their duels.

The male peacock engages in contests with other males that are based not on force but on looks; for this reason, it has developed its typical showy tail plumage.

The female reedbuck plays no role in selection of the male; she passively accepts the winner of the duel as her mate.

The peahen
The female peacock decides the winner of the display contest. In this case, the female selects the male on the basis of his physical characteristics.

 behavior can induce extensive morphological changes through that evolutionary process known as *natural selection*.

Competition among males in the polygymous species may be of two types. In the first type, only those few males that succeed in winning out over the others in combat can hope to reproduce; the males perform selection themselves. In the second, in which the females select the males, the males must take advantage of the brief courting period to prove they are healthy and possess characteristics that make them suitable for their environment and that will therefore be advantageous for their offspring. Both these forms of sexual selection have the same result—the males evolve different forms than the females. In the first case, they will be larger and sometimes have special structures useful for fighting; in the second, they will take to the extreme the features selected by the females as representative of fitness. The same thing can occur in the polyandrous species, reversing the roles of the two sexes.

Theoretically, in monogamous species, when there are equal numbers of males and females, all the individuals ought to reproduce and there should be no reason for sexual selection. However, both the males and the females may prefer mating with a member of the opposite sex that has characteristics above the average for the population. The exhibition of the male is what we call courtship; the male attempts to convince the female to accept him as her partner.

Courting also has another very important function: It permits the two sexes to recognize one another as members of the same species. If this weren't so, both would risk wasting their investment in reproduction. Hybrids—the offspring of two individuals of different species—are usually sterile. What's more, while the parents are perfectly adapted to their respective environments, the hybrids are not, since they have different characteristics than either of the parent species.

Men and women

The investment in reproduction is different for the two sexes in our species as well. The woman must go through pregnancy and the number of children

POLYGAMY IN MAN
Under special circumstances, a human society may adopt reproductive strategies that are different from those based on a family nucleus made up of a man and a woman.

The Yanomami are hunter/gatherers who live in the Amazon rain forest. According to their customs, a man is expected to have more than one wife. However, this is possible only for those men who enjoy a high social position. The result is that other men cannot marry, or can do so only much later than women do.

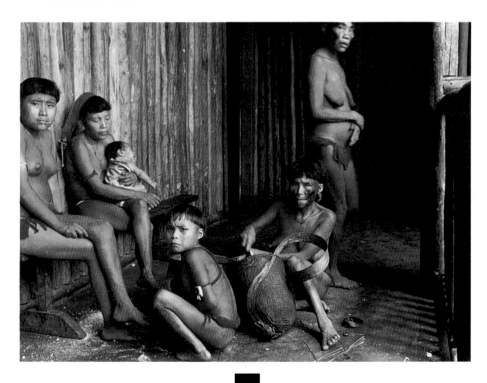

The Ladakhi are farmers/herdsmen who live in India near the Tibetan border. Their family structure has adapted to the geographical conditions, which do not permit increasing the cultivated acreage; therefore, the oldest son inherits the family land, and marries. Since there is no other available land, the other sons cannot have a family of their own; they remain with their elder brother and share a single wife.

she can bear is limited by her fertile periods; the man, on the other hand, can have a greater number of children by mating with more than one woman.

We humans have therefore compromised between caring for our offspring and the number of offspring we produce. Many of today's societies have created conditions favorable to monogamy, but we still are not sure what system was originally adopted by our species.

PARENTS AND OFFSPRING

Natural selection encourages those individuals that produce the most offspring, but also those that through a long line of descendants succeed in preserving their genes over many generations.

In some species, the parents' efforts to reproduce stop at producing gametes and fertilizing the eggs with the sperm; in others, the efforts include very lengthy periods of parental care. In the first case, the number of offspring is generally quite high, but the probability of their surviving to sexual maturity is low. Since the initial investment for the production of each single offspring is low, the death of one or more of them is not a great loss, however, and the lineage is assured.

The sperm whale, one of the largest marine mammals, up to 60 feet (18 m) in length and often weighing more than 50 tons, lives more than 70 years. The females produce only one calf at a time, and take care of it for many years.

REPRODUCTION STRATEGIES
Some animals produce many offspring, of which only a few survive. Others have few offspring but work to ensure them a high probability of survival.

The strategy of the parental-care species is different. They have few off-spring, but the probability of their surviving to reproduce is high. The parents take care of their young from the moment they are fertilized, protecting, oxygenating, or incubating the eggs in such a way as to guarantee the efficient development of the embryo.

Later, they feed their offspring and protect them from predators.

In some species with complex behaviors and good learning abilities, the parents can transmit particular behaviors to their offspring, teach them about their environment and its dangers, and generally supply the knowledge that will give them a survival advantage.

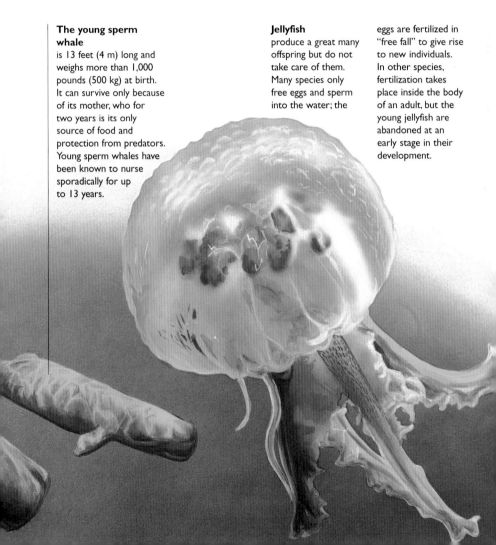

The young sperm whale
is 13 feet (4 m) long and weighs more than 1,000 pounds (500 kg) at birth. It can survive only because of its mother, who for two years is its only source of food and protection from predators. Young sperm whales have been known to nurse sporadically for up to 13 years.

Jellyfish
produce a great many offspring but do not take care of them. Many species only free eggs and sperm into the water; the eggs are fertilized in "free fall" to give rise to new individuals. In other species, fertilization takes place inside the body of an adult, but the young jellyfish are abandoned at an early stage in their development.

The rhinoceros is a large herbivore of the African savannahs. Because of their size, the adults are safe from predators, but for the young the only hope of survival is their mothers' protection.

CARING FOR THE YOUNG
There may be many different types of parental care. Some species concentrate on protecting their young from predators; others devote much time to their education.

Conflicts of interest

In most of the parental-care species, care is usually supplied by only one of the parents, rarely by both. Why is this? Wouldn't it be more advantageous for the offspring to receive the care of both parents instead of just one?

Undoubtedly it would, but we must remember who determines the type of relationship that will exist between parents and offspring. It is the parents, who unconsciously continue to act in their own interests. Even though this may seem odd, the interests of the parents do not necessarily correspond to the best interests of the offspring.

In point of fact, the parents tend simply to have a sufficient number of offspring that, given the probability of survival for each, one or more of them will reproduce in its turn to continue the parents' lineage.

This is why parental care is usually not protracted to sexual maturity but only until such a time as a reasonable compromise has been reached between the risk that the offspring will not survive alone and the advantage for the parents of being free to conceive and care for new progeny.

This optimal compromise between number of offspring and probability

The great spotted huntress
This female cheetah has survived to reproduce thanks to her hunting ability, which she owes mainly to her experience and knowledge of the prey. The female must now transmit this knowledge to her young so that they will have the tools they need to also survive.

The cheetah
is a lone hunter that relies on its own abilities to catch its fast-moving prey. At a very early age, the kittens begin following their mother as she hunts, and learn as much as they can before they are left to fend for themselves.

of survival may be different for males and females, because of their different characteristics.

As we have seen, the females generally invest more time and energy in each of their young and cannot have many. For this reason, the females are often more interested in increasing the probability of survival. In other cases, it is the male that plays this role.

Fratricide
The firstborn of a brood of Verreaux eagles is larger than its siblings and obtains more than its share of food. The other chicks become weaker and weaker and often die, sometimes from the wounds inflicted by their larger sibling. The parents do not intervene, because in this way, even if food is scarce, at least one fledgling is assured of surviving.

For example, in many fish, the males defend a territory in which they mate with the females that enter it. For them, defending the eggs is neither an added cost nor a loss of opportunity to reproduce—and it might even be that the females will be attracted by a male that already has a brood.

When a single parent cannot guarantee the survival of even a limited number of offspring, the other cooperates in providing care. This is the case with birds, which invest a great deal of energy in producing and incubating eggs that are rather large for the size of their bodies, and in providing food for the fledglings until they become independent. This is so difficult that in many species the parents, despite their working

PARENTS VS. PROGENY
Parents and their young tend to each pursue their own interests, and the parents always win out in this type of competition.

Weaning
As time passes, young baboons are denied more and more firmly by their mother, until they cannot even go near her. Obviously, it would be more convenient for the young to continue to be cared for, but at a certain point the mother finds it more advantageous to abandon them and reproduce again.

THE CARE PROVIDER
According to the needs of the
species, it can be the male,
the female, or both that
care for the young.

Mother kangaroo
This young kangaroo is
almost old enough to
leave its mother's pocket
to make room for a new
joey, but it will remain in
its mother's company for
a long time. As in most
mammals, it is the female
kangaroo that cares for
the young until their
chances of survival alone
are good.

 as a team, do not succeed in raising more than one chick at a time. What is more, in some cases, the male feeds the female in order to facilitate her work of producing eggs.

Parental care in humans

What makes us humans able to live in our environment—so much so that at least in recent history, we have been able to alter it to fit our needs—are not so much our physical characteristics as our intellectual capabilities. These permit us to achieve a high degree of cooperation with others and to learn much about the world we live in, of dangers and sources of food, and give us the ability to manufacture tools, clothing, and shelter. All this is indis-

Mother and father penguin
The emperor penguin reproduces in Antarctica in early winter. The male incubates the single egg far from the water. During this period he eats nothing and can lose up to half his body weight. Mother takes over at hatching, and the male finally goes in search of a meal. Later, both parents care for the chick until summer, when the whole family returns to the sea.

Father seahorse
As in many other fish, it is the male seahorse that cares for the young. In this species, the male protects the eggs in a special pouch on his abdomen until they hatch.

Arrow-poison frogs
live in the rain forests of South and Central America. After hatching, in some species, the father carries the tadpoles on his back, then deposits them in a stream where they complete their development.

HUMAN DEVELOPMENT AND SOCIETY

Humans have a long infancy. The length of the period of parental care varies from society to society.

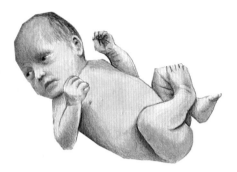

At birth, humans are completely helpless. A baby's only activity is nursing.

At one year of age, most children begin walking.

At about two, a child has all its baby teeth. It stops nursing, but must still be fed by its parents. It also begins speaking in simple phrases.

At six, the child's fast growth slows down. Its permanent teeth are beginning to come in, and its ability to communicate is well developed. At this age, the child begins to learn the cultural elements of its society as taught by the adults.

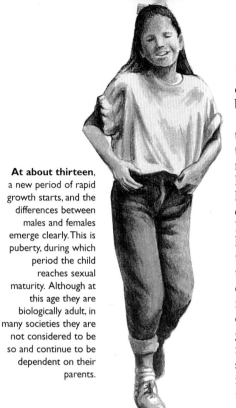

At about thirteen, a new period of rapid growth starts, and the differences between males and females emerge clearly. This is puberty, during which period the child reaches sexual maturity. Although at this age they are biologically adult, in many societies they are not considered to be so and continue to be dependent on their parents.

At twenty, growth is completed, but in many societies the cultural learning period continues, as does dependency on the adults.

pensable if we are to achieve efficiency in gathering or hunting food and in defending ourselves from danger and bad weather.

The key to success in these activities, and thus in survival, is learning, the capacity to acquire and use information. But learning takes time, and learning what we humans need to know in order to be independent in our environment takes many years. Most humans, therefore, prefer to have fewer children to care for, rather than have many they may be unable to adequately provide for. With many children, also, some parents might find it difficult to have the time to pass on information necessary for proper growth and survival. Passing on information on survival is essential to our species. The energy required for raising and educating children until the time of sexual maturity—and often beyond—is so great that the mother alone often cannot provide it. This is why in our species, both parents cooperate in providing parental care, which is different from most other mammals.

PREY AND PREDATORS

The reciprocal selection enacted by prey and predators is one of the principal forces driving evolution. The result of this process is an incredible variety of physical forms and models for interaction.

Most animals must face numerous dangers during their lives, and many of these come from other animals that want to feed at their expense. Therefore, in order to survive and reproduce, the different species have evolved suitable antipredator strategies.

For a potential prey, the best defense is to avoid being noticed by the predator. This is why some animals spend

Twig or Insect?
The strategy of the walkingstick consists of remaining immobile, so as to be mistaken for a twig and go unnoticed by predators.

Chemical warfare
The foul-smelling secretion produced by the glands of the skunk is enough to dissuade most predators from attacking this animal.

most of their time unmoving and silent in a place where they are not easily visible. This strategy is more efficient if the animal blends in well with its surroundings. Animals that use this strategy have thus evolved *protective coloring*—camouflage—that is, body colors similar to those of their surrounding environment. The limitations to this strategy, however, are many; for example, the *Lacerta viridis*, a large green lizard, is almost invisible in a field, but if it moves onto a tree trunk or if the grass turns yellow in a drought, the animal will suddenly be highly visible to a predatory bird.

Some species have perfected this strategy and have developed the ability to change the appearance of their bodies to a certain extent in order to better

HOW PREY DEFEND THEMSELVES
The strategies developed by different species to defend themselves against predators are highly varied and often surprising.

Sprinters
The only way a hare can defend itself is to outrun or outmaneuver the predator, hopefully in time to reach a safe shelter.

Armed defense
When attacked, the porcupine defends itself by hunching up. It thus shows the predator the spines on its back and protects its vulnerable underside.

A poisonous dish
Ladybugs produce a liquid that makes them inedible. Their showy colors allow predators to recognize them and so avoid the risk of being poisoned.

The prairie dog forms social groups in which the members recognize each other and defend their territory from individuals from other groups. The territorial boundaries are a group tradition and remain the same generation after generation.

The lookout
When out in the open, the members of the group take turns at guard duty.

LIVING AS PREY
For such social species as the North American black-tailed prairie dog, living in groups makes it easier to see any threats.

match the background. The chameleon is the most obvious example; the octopus, besides being able to change color, can make the surface of its body appear rippled like the sand of the sea bottom.

Other species don't even try to go unnoticed—quite the contrary, since their bright colors make them visible to predators against any background. Strangely enough, it is exactly here that the advantage lies, since these are species that are not edible or that strongly resemble inedible species. A predator that eats an inedible species associates the unpleasant experience with the color of the animal, and as a result, will avoid ani-

Alarm signals
The alarm signal sounded by the lookout is different for predators approaching on foot or overhead, and thus the members of the group have a good chance of escaping from a predator.

mals with similar coloring. The edible species capable of imitating the coloration of the poisonous ones are therefore at an advantage.

Other animals use a completely different strategy, and rely on their ability to avoid capture after having been singled out by the predator. There are species that flee until they reach a place the predator cannot go or until it is tired out. Other species stay where they are and protect themselves with special structures such as shells or spines.

Some animals have such physical characteristics as horns, fangs, claws, or simply a large size, with which they can actively defend themselves if attacked.

The chameleon approaches its prey slowly, so as not to frighten it. When it is within striking distance, it extends its sticky tongue at lightning speed to capture the prey.

In the case of the species that care for their young, one of the parents' most important roles is that of protecting their offspring.

Many species have even evolved specific alarm signals used by the parents to tell the young to run for shelter or by the young to call for help.

Safety in numbers

It can be useful for the prey to form groups. While an isolated individual that encounters a predator is certain to be attacked, this is less probable if the individual is part of a large group, since the predator will have many alternatives. What is more, the predator may

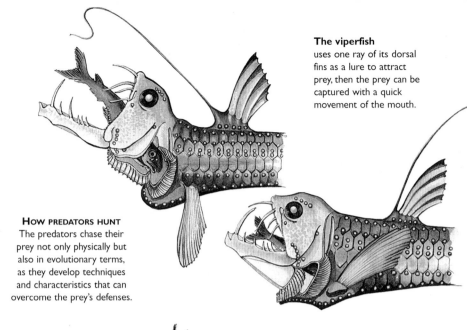

The viperfish
uses one ray of its dorsal fins as a lure to attract prey, then the prey can be captured with a quick movement of the mouth.

HOW PREDATORS HUNT
The predators chase their prey not only physically but also in evolutionary terms, as they develop techniques and characteristics that can overcome the prey's defenses.

The cheetah
This predator can run at 60 mph (100 km/h) over short distances. Its talents as a sprinter permit it to capture its principal prey: gazelles.

The gazelles are slower than the cheetah, but they have more stamina, so if the predator misses on the first try, it is probable that the gazelle will escape in a chase.

become confused when faced with a mass of moving animals in which it is difficult to distinguish one individual from another. This strategy is clear in a school of fish or a flock of birds. Also, the color patterns of many animals, such as zebras, make it difficult for a predator to single out one animal.

To the advantages offered by the group, the social species add that of cooperation. It is much harder for a predator to attack if one or another individual is always on guard, and much harder to bring down an individual if the entire group cooperates in defending it.

The predators' weapons

The prey's escape means an empty plate for the predator, and in the long run such a situation can prove fatal. For this reason, the predators must adapt their attack strategies as the prey evolves new defense mechanisms.

Both prey and predators use the same senses for locating each other and the same physical structures for attack or defense. Behaviors such as "freezing" so as not to be seen, or running, are used by both. This is not surprising if we consider that many animals are both prey and predators, depending on the circumstances. Nor is it rare that the descendants of a herbivorous species evolve carnivorous habits, and vice versa, and in these cases it is only natural that the new species should adapt the structures and behaviors of their progenitors to their new needs.

PREDATOR SOCIETIES
The African hunting dog provides an excellent example of how a social group can increase its efficiency in capturing prey. This African canid was once very numerous but is now threatened with extinction.

Why live in a pack?
The prey of the African hunting dog weigh an average 110 pounds (50 kg), enough to satisfy a pack of ten or so individuals. Cooperation is useful for defending the food from being stolen by other predators, but it is also useful for capturing large animals such as the gnu.

Hunting parties

Such behavioral characteristics as learning are generally highly developed in the large carnivores. And if it is true that cooperation can help the prey avoid the predators, it is equally true that by cooperating in the hunt, the predators can take large animals that a single individual could never hope to bring down.

In the most able species, the different members of a pack play different roles during a hunt. Some frighten the prey and direct it toward the rest of the pack waiting in ambush. After a single individual is selected and isolated, it is surrounded and killed. If the attempt is to succeed, every predator must do its part, and this does not necessarily mean attacking all together. The actual killing is simply the last action, and only a few participate in it. It is therefore extremely important that the captured prey be shared among all those that contributed to the success of the hunt.

On the prowl
African hunting dogs begin hunting at four months. When the pups are tired, the adults hide them in the bushes, safe from lions, until the hunt is over.

The youngest of the young
During hunting forays, the very young pups remain in their lairs in the care of an adult. When the hunters return, they regurgitate a part of the meat to feed those that stayed behind.

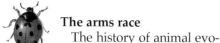

The arms race

The history of animal evolution recalls an arms race between two world powers: Each side stimulates the other to invent new and more powerful weapons and strategies. And yet the relationship between prey and predators is not as symmetrical as it might seem. Every time a predator attempts to catch a prey that escapes, there is a loser and a winner. What does each win or lose? Do the respective "prizes" have equal value? The predator's prize is a meal, while the prey, by escaping, has won its life. In other words, the risks in the two cases are very different.

Just think that there is probably no predator that at least once in its life has failed to make its catch, and that often the successful hunts are but a small percentage of all the attempts. Despite this, these individuals have survived to adulthood and have reproduced. A prey that succeeds in reproducing has not been captured; it is different from the predator, in that the prey has *never* lost. We may say, then, that whenever a predator captures a prey it is contributing to natural selection, since it eliminates an individual that was unable to escape. The result is that the predators make the prey of future generations more and more difficult to capture, and sooner or later the predators will also have to submit to selection.

The great hunter

One very special species has gone where normal predators will never

THE PREY WIN OUT
Despite appearances, the prey always have the advantage in their competition with the predators, although perhaps in numbers only, not in individual defensive mechanisms.

Who is stronger? Prey are not, as we might think, completely defenseless against the predators. Most of the time they survive the attacks, even when they would seem to be at a disadvantage. It is not unusual for a group of baboons to drive away a large leopard.

Wolves have to be very skillful in order to take musk oxen by surprise. The herd closes ranks in a defensive formation and many attempts are required before a prey can be taken.

HUMANS' MOST FEARFUL WEAPON

Social development has allowed humans to successfully compete with all other species. This characteristic is so deep-rooted that it is often applied for pure sport.

THE UNIVERSAL PREDATOR

Any species may be the prey of humans, even if this was not its role in the pre-human ecosystem. This does not occur in other predatory animals, which are generally specialized in hunting only a few prey species.

Beaters and horsemen

The human capacity for cooperation has permitted developing highly sophisticated hunting strategies, in which groups of individuals play different roles and use different tools.

The hunting horn Communication among hunters is fundamental for fluid, efficient action.

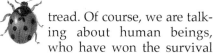

tread. Of course, we are talking about human beings, who have won the survival race with the prey hands down. We humans are such efficient killers that we have succeeded in causing the extinction of entire species. How did we succeed? Are we immune from the asymmetry between the selection operating on prey and that operating on predators? First of all, remember that humans did not evolve from a group of true predators. Excellent learning and social skills were qualities of our primate ancestors. These characteristics triggered another, much more rapid type of evolution: cultural transmission. Thanks to our culture, in only a few thousand years we humans have been able to equip ourselves with tools that natural selection never could have supplied, such as manufactured weapons like lances, bows and arrows, and rifles. Unfortunately, the natural selection that operates on other animals is not successful when it comes to avoiding bullets.

NO PLACE LIKE HOME

The characteristics of a species are suitable only for a certain environment, within which certain optimal areas exist. Each individual will therefore attempt to settle in the most favorable area for its needs, although not all succeed.

Along the long route that will culminate in reproduction, an animal has many needs; it must find the right climatic conditions, such as temperature and humidity, and sufficient food, and it must have the opportunity to mate as well as, according to the species, a place where it can raise its young or hide from predators. If these resources are not sufficient for all the individuals that are born, there will be strong competition. Those that succeed in winning a good position containing all or most of the necessary resources must also defend it from intruders that also want it. The environment in

FEEDING TERRITORIES
The red fox is an opportunist, a species capable of exploiting the many different kinds of resources found in its environment. These resources must be defended from other individuals, and are thus included in territories protected by individual animals.

Territorial expansion
In undisturbed conditions, the territory of a fox is generally from 75 to 3,700 acres (30 to 1,500 ha), depending mainly on the availability of food. If food is scarce, the animal can find enough only in a larger territory.

which a species can live will thus be divided into various bordering territories, areas defended by individuals against other individuals.

The sizes of territories vary. First of all, the more resources the animal needs, the larger its territory will have to be. The more abundant the resource with respect to needs, however, the smaller the territories will be, until, in the case of practically unlimited resources with respect to consumption, there is no longer any need for individual territories to exist. Wouldn't it be more advantageous to have a large territory and therefore more resources?

The fox and humans
The fox is an animal that seems to tolerate human activity well, and even to profit by it. The garbage produced in urban areas provides these animals with a good source of food. It has been observed that the territories near garbage dumps are rather small; those further away are much larger.

Food and territory
The map shows the location of the foxes and the width of their territories around a plentiful food source.

The problem is that, as the territory expands so do its borders, and therefore the effort required to defend them. Animals always try to avoid expending energy uselessly, so they compromise between the quantity of resources and the energy needed to defend them.

The smallest territories in proportion to the size of the animal exist when they do not contain any real resource but guarantee only a breeding ground.

This is the case, for example, with species in which the males fight to gain possession of a small area in which they mate if a female enters it.

How does the occupant of a territory defend it from intruders? This is quite simple in the case of the small territories used for reproduction, which are continually defended through physical combat, since when they defend their territories or challenge an occupant, the animals' entire attention is focused on reproduction alone. On the other hand, the animals that have very extensive territories in which they carry on all their activities, including the search for food, cannot devote all their time to active defense of their frontiers. It is therefore more convenient to give warning signals that tell an intruder it is entering an occupied territory.

This system is very useful for both the individual residing in the territory and that nearing the border. If the latter is the occupant of a bordering territory, it is an advantage to avoid entering the

BREEDING GROUNDS
Some species defend an area not for the food it contains but because it is indispensable for reproduction.

Lesser black-backed gulls nest in large colonies, but each pair of birds defends only a small space in which they lay their eggs and raise their young.

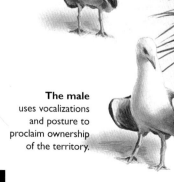

The male uses vocalizations and posture to proclaim ownership of the territory.

Birds-of-paradise
The males defend an area in which they conduct their courtship displays with the aim of attracting females.

The challenger When another male comes too close, the result is a fight, even though it is rarely bloody.

KEEPING ONE'S DISTANCE
According to what they
are defending and their species'
capacity for communication,
animals use different signals to
tell other individuals that a
territory is occupied and that
they are not welcome.

The robin
advertises its
presence and emits
sound signals.

The fox,
like many other
mammals, relies mainly
on olfactory signals to
mark the boundaries
of its territory.

territory of its neighbor and finding itself forced to fight. This is also true for an individual that does not have a territory, such as a young animal looking for a home, which finds it useful to know whether or not an area is occupied. Marking borders, therefore, avoids useless and wasteful combat, which will then be carried on only with the real intruders that ignore the warning signals.

Many types of signals are used for marking borders, depending on what is recognizable and can be produced by the species in question, for example, mammals, with their highly developed sense of smell, use mainly chemical substances produced by special glands.

On the move

It is rare for an animal to live out its entire life in the area in which it was born. Often, at least one phase of its life involves a move, which may happen for a number of reasons.

The most common type of movement is *dispersion*, in which, usually, young individuals are looking for a territory of their own. In the species that practice parental care, the young are forcibly expelled from the area occupied by the parents or the group if the parents or groups do not have sufficient resources for supporting all the young produced by all the adults

The stag
vocalizes and also leaves olfactory signals on the branches of trees.

The lynx
uses some visual signals to mark its territory.

DISPERSION

As in many other species, the young of the beaver do not live out their lives where they were born.

House hunting

Most of the young set out from the territory of the colony to look for new territories when they are less than a year old. As they are moving around, these individuals are easy prey and few reach adulthood.

Dam builders

Beavers live in ponds that offer good shelter from land-based predators. Often the animals themselves create artificial ponds by building dams from pieces of wood they cut with their powerful incisors.

THE BEAVER COMMUNITY
Beavers live in small colonies in
which only one pair reproduces.
They defend their territories from
intruders with great ferocity.

during their reproductive lives.

The dispersal of the young has another important purpose: to reduce the probability that two related individuals will meet and mate. Mating between close relatives can generate young that are not perfectly healthy, in other words, with low chances of survival.

This occurs because each individual has two copies of the genes contained in the DNA, the molecule that contains all the information needed to develop physical and behavioral characteristics. One of these copies is inherited from the mother, the other from the father. In the case where there is a defect in the genetic information received from one parent, the "good" information received from the other parent will probably be sufficient to produce a completely normal individual. But if the parents are related, it is more probable that the DNA of both may carry the same defect, inherited from a common ancestor. If both parents transmit the faulty copy to their young, they will have two copies of the defective gene and none that can compensate, and will consequently have dysfunctions.

For this reason, expelling the young from the group is an advantage for both the parents and the offspring, since all involved will benefit from a healthy lineage and sufficient resources for reproduction.

In some social species that live in groups and do not have a fixed territory, the same result is achieved by expelling only the males, while the

FLEXIBLE TERRITORIALITY
When food resources are scarce or variable, the territorial system may be either partially or totally abandoned. This is the case with the gnu.

DURING MIGRATION
the males are forced to move their territories. The territories become smaller and disappear altogether if the herd is constantly moving.

INDIVIDUAL TERRITORIES
The males each defend a territory in which they court the females. The territories of the members of a settled herd are 330 to 490 feet (100 to 150 m) in diameter.

females remain in the group. In these species, the two sexes never live together and meet only during the mating season.

Most of the young animals that disperse do not live long enough to reproduce. The limited resources available in an area are not sufficient to support more than a certain number of individuals, and for this reason a young animal can have its own territory only if it conquers it by defeating a weaker individual, usually older than itself.

In all cases, the young that are dispersing are an easier target for predators, since they are inexpert and their physical prowess and/or defensive structures are not fully developed.

In exceptional cases, major changes in the environment can allow a species to move beyond the area it previously occupied. This happens when the level of the sea rises and two basins that were previously separated by land come into contact, but it also occurs the other way around, when the seas recede and open paths from the continents to the islands or other continents. In these cases, the young will be able to disperse and establish new territories until the new area is completely occupied.

Migration

Another type of movement is *migration*. Different from dispersion, migration

The gnu
is an African antelope that lives in very large herds that may settle in a single area or make long seasonal migrations on circular itineraries, depending on available pastures.

is an event in which the majority, if not all, of the population participates and the movement is not casual; it has a precise destination and calls for return to the point of departure. For example, a population may move continually along a circular path, following a source of food. Or migration may consist of fast travel between two areas, which may be very distant from one another, with long stays in each. This is what happens in species that spend the winter and the summer in different areas in order to best exploit the resources of each area.

Other species do not make seasonal migrations but instead return to their place of birth only to reproduce, after having spent long growth periods in areas more suitable for that purpose.

Reproduction is without a doubt a very important factor in migrations. The young sometimes have special needs that can be met only in a certain environment. Even when this is not the case, the parents are driven by the need to nourish their offspring to reproduce during a time of the year and in a place where food is abundant.

How do the migratory animals find their way? The problem is by no means simple, if we remember that the individuals of some species always return to reproduce in exactly the same place and that in other species, years go by before the individuals reach sexual maturity and return to their place of birth.

In order to do all this, it is not enough to know how to keep on a straight course; it is also necessary for

MIGRATION
The species that have the ability to cover great distances may derive advantages from visiting different areas according to their needs.

The humpback whale may grow as long as 43 feet (13 m) and weigh 30 tons. Like many other large cetaceans, these animals spend the winters in tropical waters, off the coast of Colombia, for example, where the females give birth to their young and mate with the males.

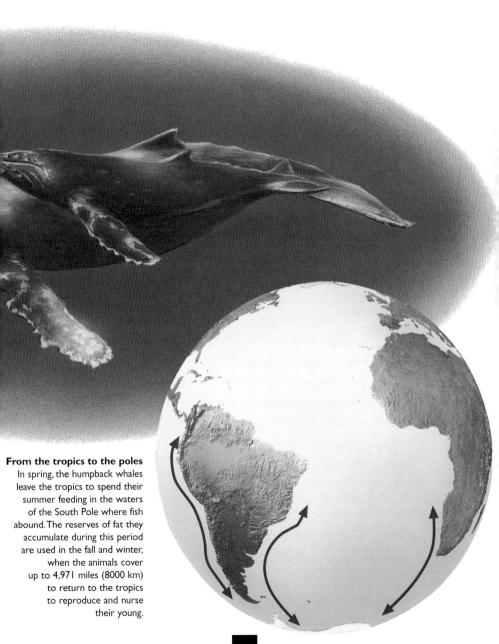

From the tropics to the poles
In spring, the humpback whales leave the tropics to spend their summer feeding in the waters of the South Pole where fish abound. The reserves of fat they accumulate during this period are used in the fall and winter, when the animals cover up to 4,971 miles (8000 km) to return to the tropics to reproduce and nurse their young.

the animal to know its position with respect to its destination. It is as though we were in a vast desert, looking for the only oasis. If the only instrument we have is a compass, we can hold a straight course and not go around in circles, but it is unlikely we will find the oasis unless we have a map that gives us both its position and ours. It has been found that some animals are capable of finding their direction on the basis of such reference points as the sun, the stars, and the earth's magnetic field, but it is harder to imagine how they can draw themselves a "map."

Humans' territories

Like many other primates, we humans are social animals. We originally lived in tribal groups, made

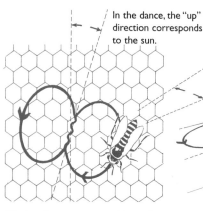

Homing pigeons seem to draw up a sort of "olfactory map" on the basis of the odors borne on the wind to the pigeon loft. It seems that the characteristic odor of the area in which they find themselves gives them their position with respect to their home loft. They are also able to use the sun and the earth's magnetic field to navigate.

In the dance, the "up" direction corresponds to the sun.

The inclination of the main part of the dance gives the direction of the source of food with respect to the sun.

The bees move their abdomens and emit more or less rapid-fire sounds to indicate the distance of the source of food from the hive.

Worker bees Once a source of food is discovered, the workers return to the hive and communicate the information to the other workers by performing a special figure-eight dance on the walls of the combs.

Sea turtles travel for thousands of miles to return to the beaches on which they were born. It has been shown that these animals can perceive two different characteristics of the earth's magnetic field, which, taken together, pinpoint an area, rather like map coordinates. It may be that thanks to the magnetic field the sea turtles understand where they are with respect to their destination.

NAVIGATION AND ORIENTATION

Animals that travel great distances use different mechanisms to find their way. These vary with species and needs, and many are still mysterious.

The American eel makes migrations of about 620 miles (1,000 km). This fish has receptors along its body that are very sensitive to electrical fields, in particular those generated as the ocean currents move water through the earth's magnetic field. It has been suggested that its electrical receptors act as navigational instruments.

Roots
About 100,000 years ago, a part of Africa was inhabited by human beings that were at least physically similar to modern humans.

EUROPE, ASIA, AND OCEANIA
It was probably improvements in tool-making, transportation, navigation, and language that allowed humans to expand into the rest of Africa, Europe, Asia, and Oceania over a period of about 65,000 years.

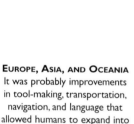 up of a few dozen people each, that occupied and defended a more or less permanent territory according to the availability of environmental resources. The early tribal groups lived in constant tension with the other tribes nearby, with which they had only sporadic contact.

Things began to change when agriculture developed and more efficient weapons were invented. The populations began to be organized into vast kingdoms that conducted trade with

HUMAN DISPERSION
Humans are distributed over almost all of the earth's dry land. As with other species, this spread was often encouraged by environmental changes as well as by the ability of humans to solve the problems of survival and travel.

The Americas
Expansion into the Americas became possible only when humans developed the skills needed to travel in inhospitable lands and to produce clothing for protection against the cold, and because of favorable conditions for crossing the Bering Strait that separates Asia from North America.

one another until today when people engage in free trade.

Does the idea of territory make sense anymore? What has remained of the ancient defense behavior? Maybe much more than we think. Maybe it surfaces every time we think about our fellow humans as "us" and "them," or when we lock the door of our house to protect what's inside it.

SOCIAL BEHAVIOR

Animals are constantly competing, especially if they are members of the same species. In many cases, however, cooperating is more advantageous than going it alone, and many species have developed specific behaviors that encourage cooperation.

Many animals have few contacts with other members of their species. Sometimes, two individuals that meet may ignore one another, mate, or fight, either for a mate or for possession of certain resources. In the species that care for their young, the relationship with the offspring is usually more lasting, as it is with the partner that contributes to raising the young, but in any case these interactions can come to an end

The salpa
is a warm water stockfish that lives in schools. The numbers and the coloration of these fish can confuse predators and give the individuals a higher chance of survival.

SPECIFIC AND INTERSPECIFIC INTERACTION
The individuals of many species live together with other individuals of the same or other species, and interact in various ways.

Cleaner fish
Some fish specialize in removing parasites from larger fish, which visit the "cleaning stations" on a regular basis. For the cleaners, the parasites are a source of food, so this relationship is advantageous for both species.

when their purpose is fulfilled. A permanent group will often be formed only if it represents a means for resolving survival problems that persist over time. For example, as we have seen, certain animals live in groups made up of many individuals in order to lessen the probability of being captured by a predator, but even in this case, there may be no active interaction between the individuals. A further increase in efficiency can come about only through active cooperation—when the members of a group act in such a way that all of the individual actions, which may be ineffec-

The corals are colonies made up of many polyps. All the individuals originated from a single coral polyp through asexual reproduction; the components of the colony are not even completely separated physically.

Clown fish, protected because of their distinctive swimming pattern as well as by chemicals in their mucous coat, protect the anemone from butterflyfish, which feed upon them. They also preen the anemones' tentacles to keep them free of debris and in good condition for prey capture.

tual if taken alone, solve a common problem. In other words, each individual gives up an immediate benefit to receive a greater benefit as the result of teamwork. This is the case, for example, with the different roles played by the great predators during a hunt.

The key to cooperation is efficient interaction among the members of a group. This means that each individ-ual must understand something of what the others are doing and what its role is in the current activity. In order to be able to do this, the individuals must first be able to recognize one another, so that they can distinguish strangers from the members of their social group. The group must in fact present a united front and help each other defend the group's resources from other groups.

INSECT SOCIETIES

Social insects include termites, ants, and some bees and wasps. These species form societies in which reproduction is the prerogative of a few individuals, while the others are sterile and divided into specialized categories called castes or classes.

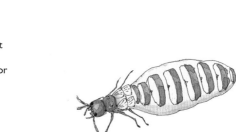

The soldiers
specialize in the defense of the colony, thanks to their peculiar physical structure and behavior.

The workers
The most numerous caste is that of the workers, individuals of both sexes, or in some insects, single-sexed, that see to the needs of the colony, from searching for food to feeding the nymphs, the newborn individuals that do not yet work.

The reproductive caste
consists of a queen and a king. There may also be secondary reproductives.

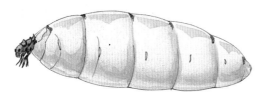

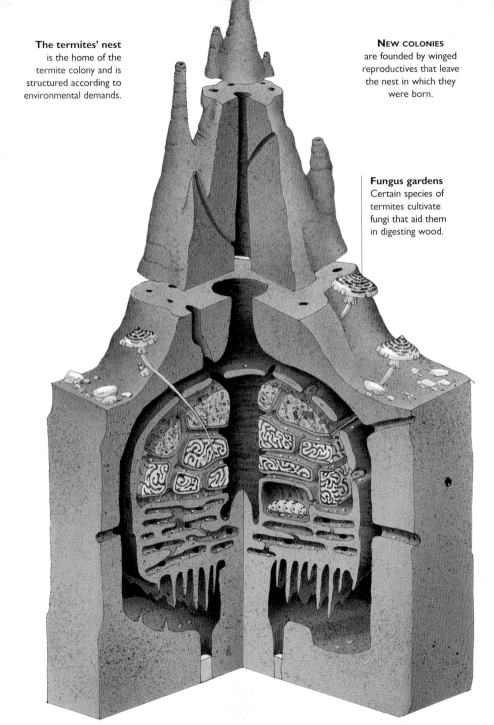

The termites' nest is the home of the termite colony and is structured according to environmental demands.

NEW COLONIES are founded by winged reproductives that leave the nest in which they were born.

Fungus gardens Certain species of termites cultivate fungi that aid them in digesting wood.

Social organization

Competition also exists within societies. The individuals act for the good of the group, but only because they benefit individually from it. Sometimes, an individual will seem to be attempting to monopolize as many resources as possible, but most species have no choice in these matters, especially non-mammals. There is, of course, a limit to competition, since one individual cannot go so far as to deprive other individuals of the resources they need, or the group will break up. For example, the members of a social group cannot do without food and a place to hide from predators. On the other hand, they can exist without

WHEN SOCIAL BEHAVIOR IS AN ADVANTAGE
Not like individuals in the wild, stray cats in cities have food available in certain known places. These cats organize territorial groups and adopt social behavior patterns.

Female cats
Friendly relationships among females are frequent. A few days after giving birth, the mother cat tends to put all the kittens in a single place, far from the boundaries of the territory, near sources of food, and with many hiding places. Here, the females cooperate by taking turns caring for the kittens, apparently without distinguishing between their own and those of others.

In the wild
Wild or abandoned cats in the wild must hunt to eat, and since their catch is generally sufficient only for themselves, they live solitary lives.

Tomcats
The relationships among males, as opposed to relationships among females or between females and males, is not friendly. Despite this, males generally tolerate one another and their fighting is ritualized, based on posture, expression, and vocalizations. Violent physical contact is rare.

reproducing for a certain period, and it is for this reason that reproduction—or access to a sexual partner—is the object of most competition. The result is that some individuals forego reproduction, at least for a while.

Often only one or a few individuals of one sex reproduce, usually males. When this type of predominance is established in both sexes, a single male and a single female will become the only reproducers of the group. In the species in which the females live with the young in groups apart from the males, the sexes come into contact only in the breeding season. It may then happen that the male that wins the competitions will control all the females in the group for the reproductive season, and form a harem.

Reproductive hierarchies are very simple: The winners of the competitions mate, the others do not. Within the group, however, there also exists the need to know which individuals will have access before others to certain other resources, such as food. There is thus created a hierarchy of all the individuals. Through play, when they are young, and then with more or less violent combat, each finds its place within the social group; subordinates and superiors are established. It is essential that the animals of these species be able to memorize the individuals with which they have fought and what the outcome was, so as not to have to waste time and energy every time they encounter another member of the group. Even in this way, however, the hierarchical order is

THE STRUCTURE OF A TROOP
The hamadryas is a large African ground-dwelling monkey. As in other social species, each individual has its own place in the group hierarchy.

The gregarious males
In some cases, a young male is accepted as a follower by the dominant male, and may even be permitted to mate. As the young male matures, he begins to adopt and raise young females, thus laying the bases for his harem.

The females
are completely submissive
to the dominant male,
and are punished if they
stray too far.

The male hamadryas
control harems of females.
A band is composed of
males and their females, and
all its members cooperate
in procuring food. The bands
join together in troops, each
of which occupies a shelter
in which the monkeys spend
the night.

anything but stable; all that is needed to upset it is a death, new births, or individuals in search of promotion.

If every time this happened there were fights among all the members, the group would dissolve in short order. In the social species, the problem has been resolved by ritualizing the combats—making them as harmless as possible until in some cases they have become no more than mere visual or auditory exhibitions.

Obviously, this system can work only if the exhibitions in question

Wolves

A subordinate wolf will adopt a peculiar, somewhat crouching stance, and with its ears and tail lowered will lick the muzzle of the dominant individual. This behavior is typical of cubs begging for food, and is used by the adults as an appeasement ritual.

Chimpanzees

For chimps, parasites are a major health problem. It is solved through reciprocal grooming, which permits eliminating the parasites from the parts of the body an individual cannot reach by itself.

Grooming

The members of the group use this behavior as a tool for strengthening social cohesion and for peace-making. For instance, if one individual wants to avoid being attacked by another, it may use particular sounds to offer to groom the aggressor.

THE RITUALS
Many social species have typical rituals used by the members of the group to communicate among themselves.

The loser
If matters result in a fight, the loser can avoid being killed by assuming a position of total vulnerability in order to placate the aggressiveness of the winner.

 reflect the real capabilities of the individuals. For example, a few looks and movements may suffice for two adversaries to understand which is the stronger, with no need for coming to blows. Threatening behavior has the same purpose: One individual informs another that it will be attacked unless it immediately stops its aggressive behavior.

If matters finally result in a fight, the loser can avoid being killed by exhibit-ing the submissive behavior typical of each species that tells the winner that the loser accepts defeat and is ready to resume its place in the hierarchy. Killings within a group are rare. The exception is the case in which a male from outside the group defeats the leader and then kills all the offspring of that male. This happens because, by eliminating the young, the new leader makes their mothers available for mating again and therefore promotes

Expressions

In primates, the face is fundamental to social relations. It identifies the individual and permits the production of many visual signals thanks to the animals' capacity for facial expression.

COMMUNICATION IN SOCIETIES

There are many ways of communicating in animal societies. The codes may be based on signals of various types, from chemical to auditory.

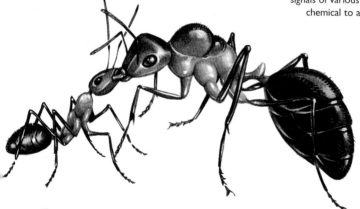

Ants

Odor and the movement of their antennas permit ants to identify other members of their anthill. The individuals also continually exchange regurgitated food so that the chemical messages it contains will spread throughout the entire anthill.

production of its own offspring, at the expense of those of its predecessor.

All behaviors relating to social life are highly complex and must be accurately expressed by the individuals in order to guarantee their permanent place in the group. Many social species have instinctive skills, thanks to which they can enact and memorize complicated interactions with other individuals.

Castes and classes

There also exist other types of societies, such as those of the insects, in which the members are divided into castes—distinct categories according to physical aspect and behavior. This type of social order is extremely inflexible

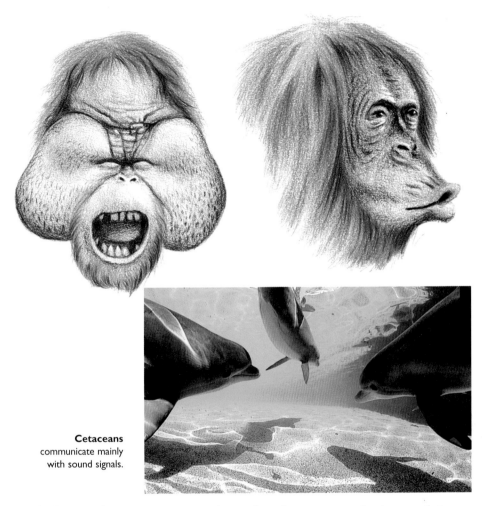

Cetaceans communicate mainly with sound signals.

and allows only one or at most a few individuals to reproduce, while the majority have no offspring and are specialized for other tasks. Many of the animals that live in castes have roles that are assigned to them from birth by rigid genetic or physiological features.

Human society

Thanks to our considerable skill in learning, communicating, and transmitting cultural information, we human beings have been able to divide up the activities required for the survival of the group into many tasks, somewhat like the specializations of the castes of the social insects. But unlike these and other social species, in human society it is sometimes possible to shift from one role to another

THE FAMILY
In humans, the family is the basic social unit. Each family nucleus is in contact with others, which may be the same or change with time according to the number of persons in the society as a whole.

THE HUMAN GROUP
The interactions among members of human societies are not unlike those in the other social species.

Social cohesion
is guaranteed by friendly gestures such as smiles and, above all, physical contact.

Communication is a fundamental element in human social interaction. Verbal language is extremely complex and is the primary means of communication. Gestures and facial expression are also very important.

with relative ease. This makes human groups very flexible, as is demonstrated by the many kinds of social structures of our present and our past history.

Despite their great differences, the various human societies all have one common characteristic: The basic unit of the group is the family, generally made up of two parents and their offspring, even though in a polygamous society one of the two adults may be part of more than one family nucleus. These nuclei seem to have been originally grouped into tribes of 80 to 120 individuals, each of whom interacted personally with all the others.

Recently, however, this situation has changed. While technological progress has led to the formation of societies made up of millions of individuals, our capacity for social interaction has not changed much. Therefore, each of us tends to maintain close contact with a number of persons who are more or less equal to the number of members in an old tribe, and to consider all the others strangers.

Social hierarchies exist where there is a separation of roles, which are very diversified especially in the industrialized societies. The stances, ways of speaking, and overall demeanor of subordinate individuals are, in many cases, very different from those of the dominant individual.

ALTRUISM

Why does altruism exist? If the primary interest of each individual is to have progeny, why do the members of some species spend time and effort or even sacrifice their own reproduction in favor of others?

The members of the social species receive an advantage from forming groups and dividing up their work, and this is true regarding reproduction as well. One might expect there to be a certain "rotation," so that every individual would be able to reproduce, but in many animal societies the majority of the individuals do not reproduce at all, or, at best do so only with difficulty.

This happens with the social insects; the majority of the group is made up of the so-called workers, sterile individuals whose work guarantees the smooth operation of all aspects of society, including the reproduction of a small number of "kings" and "queens." Even in some species that care for their young, the associa-

Sex in bees
Like other insects, bees possess a special mechanism for determining sex. If, before laying an egg, the queen fertilizes it with the sperm a male left her at the time of mating, a female will hatch. If the egg is not fertilized, the newborn bee will be a male with only one set of genes.

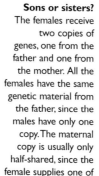

Sons or sisters?
The females receive two copies of genes, one from the father and one from the mother. All the females have the same genetic material from the father, since the males have only one copy. The maternal copy is usually only half-shared, since the female supplies one of the two copies she

possesses. "Sisters," therefore, have an average of 75 percent genetic material in common, while they will share only half with their male offspring. It is probably for this reason that the workers sacrifice their own reproduction to help the queen produce other sisters, including the new queens.

tion among individuals is composed of a reproductive nucleus—one or both parents plus the offspring—and other individuals whose only task is to help the reproductive individuals raise their young. These altruistic behaviors may seem to bring only disadvantages to those that express them, since they do not permit them to continue their line. It is also difficult, at first glance, to understand how they evolved. If a behavior exists among the individuals of a species, it must have been inherited from their ancestors, which is con-

The drones are male bees. Their only role is to mate with a female after both have left the hive of their birth.

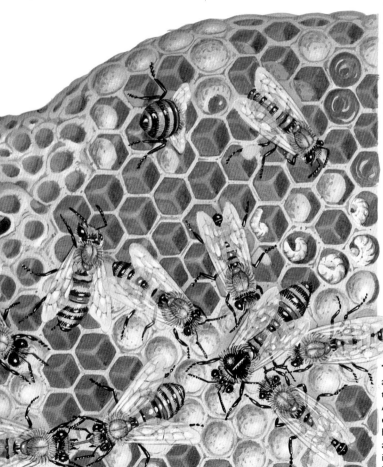

The workers are sterile females that perform all the work of the hive, from collecting food to building the cells. The workers forego reproduction in favor of the queens.

The queens are the only females that reproduce. A queen may establish a new hive after having abandoned the one in which she was born and mated.

sistent with the theory of natural selection. But how can a behavior that hinders the reproduction of those that possess it be transmitted to future generations?

Egotistical altruism

Having offspring is not the only way to transmit one's characteristics to future generations. The genes of an individual are shared by its relatives, such as parents and siblings, so helping them reproduce is equivalent to reproducing through them, even if only in part. This is the reason why we often observe altruism among closely related individuals. In some species, the effort involved in raising the

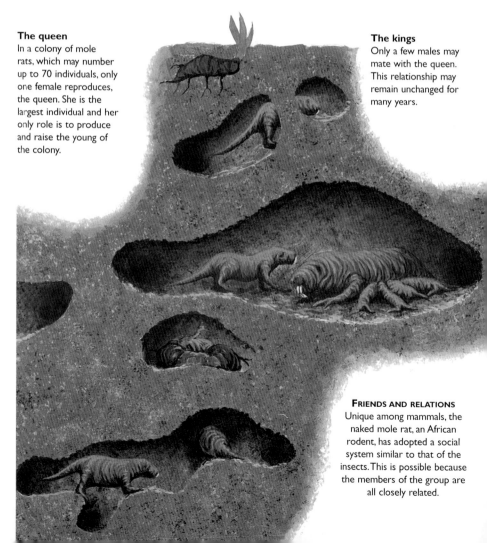

The queen
In a colony of mole rats, which may number up to 70 individuals, only one female reproduces, the queen. She is the largest individual and her only role is to produce and raise the young of the colony.

The kings
Only a few males may mate with the queen. This relationship may remain unchanged for many years.

FRIENDS AND RELATIONS
Unique among mammals, the naked mole rat, an African rodent, has adopted a social system similar to that of the insects. This is possible because the members of the group are all closely related.

young is considerable, and a pair of parents alone might not be able to achieve satisfactory results. Therefore, it may be more advantageous for an inexpert adult to reproduce indirectly by helping its parents raise new offspring, and in the meantime acquire experience, rather than to attempt to reproduce itself with little chance of success. With more expertise, it will become more advantageous for the individual to generate its own young. For this reason, in order to develop a behavior by which an individual favors the reproduction of others over its own, close relatives must be the ones to benefit, such cooperation must considerably increase the chance of

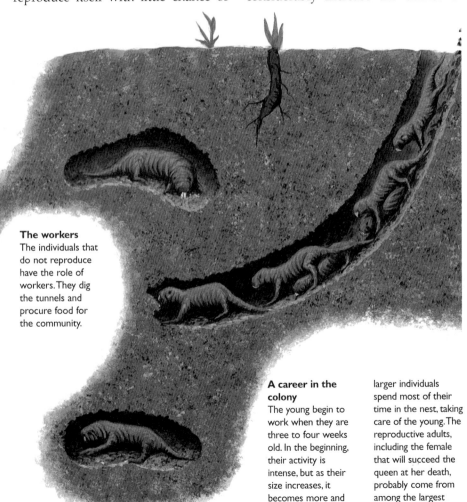

The workers
The individuals that do not reproduce have the role of workers. They dig the tunnels and procure food for the community.

A career in the colony
The young begin to work when they are three to four weeks old. In the beginning, their activity is intense, but as their size increases, it becomes more and more sporadic. The larger individuals spend most of their time in the nest, taking care of the young. The reproductive adults, including the female that will succeed the queen at her death, probably come from among the largest adults.

A GOOD INVESTMENT
Baboons can make alliances for exchanging favors.

The femme fatale
A female in estrus—ready to mate—is a coveted prize for the males of the group.

The victim
Apparently, a male has succeeded in winning possession of a female thanks to his greater physical prowess with respect to the other males.

The matchmaker
The lieutenant male seems not to derive any advantage from having helped another to mate. He expends energy and risks being wounded in the fight with the dominant male, but gets nothing in exchange. Later, however, the lieutenant may be able to obtain the help of the other male, with the roles reversed. Thus, their alliance favors both parties.

survival of the young, and direct reproduction must offer a low probability of success.

There are also cases in which the help is not directed toward a relative. This can occur in species with high learning capacities, in which the individuals recognize one another and memorize their interactions. In these cases, an individual can help another in the hope that, later, that other will exchange favors. This is a kind of cooperation in which the effects are not instantaneous but rather distributed over time.

The ability to memorize events is important not only for remembering to whom the favor must be returned, but also who owes favors, so as to maintain a balance between what has been given and what is received in exchange. If the individual that receives help does not want to return it, the others will no longer offer assistance and the individual in question

Mutual aid

An individual in trouble is always helped by the other members of its group. If the animal dies, the others do not abandon it before having tried repeatedly to rouse it.

Adoption

Young females without offspring often help other females care for their young. If the mother dies, the calf may be adopted by one of these "aunts."

will be unable to satisfy its needs.

In the social species in which the offspring require special care and protection, it is common to see the young of various mothers raised all together. In some cases, a young one whose mother has died may even be adopted. This type of altruism is more common when the members of the group are closely related. Another type of behavior in species with close and lasting relationships among the individuals is generalized help in the case of illnesses or injuries. It is clearly advantageous for all the members to display this behavior, since each individual may need help sooner or later.

On the basis of what we have said above, it does not seem possible that a

Elephants usually help even those
individuals from which they can
receive nothing in exchange, at
least in the short term. This
behavior is probably due to the
fact that the members of the herd
are closely related.

truly altruistic behavior—one that procures no advantages but represents
only an outlay of time and energy—
can evolve and persist in a species,
since it will be eliminated early in the
game by natural selection.

Any inherited behavior will continue down through the generations
only if it can provide benefits, and
what we call altruism is no exception.

Altruism in humans

We are accustomed to thinking of
altruism as one of the most noble characteristics of our species, by definition,
behavior that has no ulterior purposes.
How does this idea go along with the
lack of true altruism in other animals?
First, we must see if human altruism is
comparable to that of other species; if it
procures material advantages for the

giver as well as the receiver. Therefore, we must ask ourselves who we are willing to help, and in what circumstances.

Even those of us who live in huge metropolises tend to consider ourselves members of a more limited clan composed of the people with whom we are in daily contact, as in the tribal groups of old. We humans often take an active interest in the fate of our siblings, cousins, and other relatives, and of our closest friends. But in tribal culture, the latter figures probably coincided with the former. It is less common for people to be interested in those they have never seen, for example, people they have only heard about. This recalls the altruism exhibited toward relatives and reciprocal altruism among the members of a herd or pack, but as we have seen, such behavior also has advantages for the giver.

One important exception is adoption, or caring for a child as if it were our own. This phenomenon also exists in other animals and it is generally observed in groups in which the members are closely related. Remember, however, that this was the original condition of the human race and it is quite possible that a behavior developed in the past could have survived down to our times.

Another form of assistance extended to strangers is social security and social medicine (in some countries), but sooner or later everyone will need such help, which thus also falls under the heading of reciprocal altruism. Sometimes assistance seems to be one-way

ASSISTANCE AMONG HUMANS
The complex structure of human society and available technology have produced a high degree of reciprocal assistance by society at large to individuals in need.

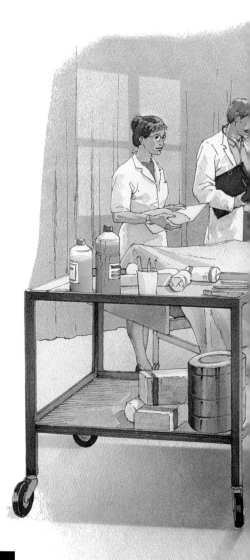

Professional assistance
Assistance can be given by individuals acting in their roles in the community, as a source of social integration, or for simple personal satisfaction.

Good neighbors
A patient we know personally may receive better than average care and attention. Humans, like other mammals, tend to help the members of their own group before others.

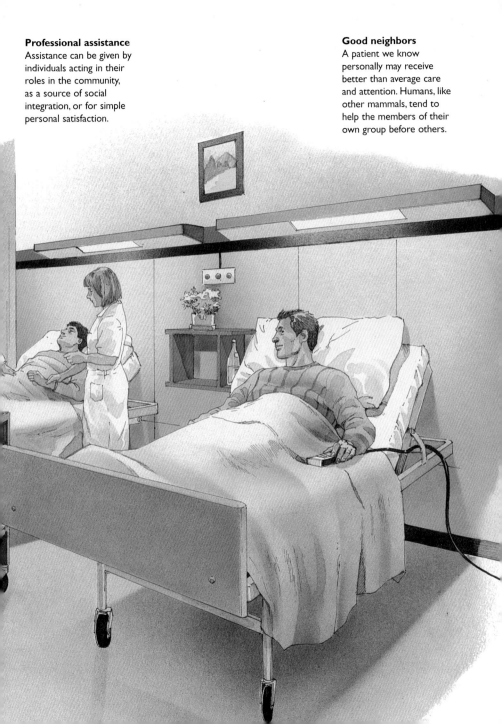

INTERSPECIES ALTRUISM

One peculiar feature of humans is that we extend our own patterns of altruistic behavior to other species, either as individuals or collectively.

The giant panda has become the symbol of the conservation of the species threatened with extinction due to the activities of humans; and as such, it is protected and assisted.

and provided to perfect strangers, such as donations of money by well-to-do individuals to help the needy. Do these philanthropists really receive nothing in exchange? There is an advantage in these cases as well, since generally those who act altruistically are well regarded. Politicians are aware of this and near election time often conduct campaigns in favor of the disadvantaged members of society.

More in general, in a cooperative species such as ours, it is indispensable to become integrated and to be appreciated within the social structure. This can stimulate anyone to perform an altruistic action with the conscious or unconscious hope of winning the approval of the other members of the clan.

Thus we may say that the attitudes that encourage altruism evolved to procure an advantage for an individual, directly or through his or her acquaintances. Human beings, alone among animals and thanks to cultural influences and the changes that have come about in our social structures, have proved capable of applying these patterns even when they do not lead to a clear advantage.

The Arabian oryx
This antelope is extinct in nature because of human hunting, but humans have nevertheless taken charge of the survival of the species; individuals were raised in zoos and after many years, a group was reintroduced into its natural habitat in a specially created park on the Arabian peninsula.

VETERINARY MEDICINE
The concern of humans with other animals does not stop at species preservation but also extends to providing care for individuals, even those not threatened with extinction, and especially if they have a strong emotional impact on humans.

Index

A

Abruzzi shepherd dog,
30–31
Acquired behavior, 17–18
Adoption, 114, 116
Advertising, 51
African hunting dog, 72–73
Alarm signals, 69
Alternative behaviors, 36
Altruism, 108–119
  egotistical, 110–111
  humans, 115–117
  interspecies, 118–119
American eel, 90
Annelid, 21
Antelopes, 46–47
Ants, 104
Arabian Oryx, 119
Arrow-poison frogs, 63
Artificial selection, 30

B

Baboons, 112–113
Bats, 4
Beaters, 76
Beaver, 84
Bees, 90
  queen, 108–109
  sex, 108–109
Behavior:
  alternative, 36
  complex, 18–20
  courtship, 50–54
  cultural transmission, 32
  definition, 4, 8
  description, 10
  evolution, 26–35
  feeding, 37
  human, 24–25
  inborn, 17–18
  innate, 17–18
  instinctual, 16–17
  learned, 17–18
  mechanisms, study of,
  8–9

seasonal, 36–43
simple, 20
social, 94–107
study of, 4–15
Birds, 17
  cuckoo, 22–23
  great crested grebe, 50
  jacana, 49
  lesser black backed gulls,
  80
  limpkin, 48
  peacock, 52
  peahen, 53
  penguin, 63
  pigeon, 27, 90
  robin, 82
  verreaux eagle, 60
  white stork, 38–39
  woodpecker, 27
  finch, 19
Birds-of-Paradise, 81
Birdsong, 22
Bivalves, 20
Body language, 24–25
Bull elephant, 37
Butterfly fish, 95

C

Camouflage, 67
Carapaces, 26
Castes, 104–105
Cats, 98–99
  cheetah, 59, 70–71
  lion, 16
  lynx, 82
  tom, 99
Cetaceans, 29, 105
Chameleon, 68, 70
Cheetah, 59, 70–71
Chimpanzees, 8, 102
Chlamydosaurus, 19
Circadian rhythms, 42
Cities, 42
Classes, 104–105
Cleaner fish, 94

Clown fish, 95
Cohesion, social, 106
Color, 8
  protective, 66
Communication, 34,
  104–107
  alarm signals, 69
  body language, 24–25
  facial expressions, 104–105
  hunters, 77
Competition, 14
Complex behaviors, 18–20
Conclusions, 7
Cooperation, 94
Corals, 95
Courtship behavior, 50–54
Cuckoo, 22–23
Culture:
  technological, 35
  transmission of behavior,
  32
  tribal, 35
Cycles:
  circadian rhythms, 42
  human, 41–43
  seasonal, 38

D

Density, population, 40
Deep-sea angler, 20
Development:
  human, 64–65
  social, 76
Dispersion, 83–85
  human, 92–93
DNA, 18, 31, 85
Dogs:
  Abruzzi shepherd,
  30–31
  African hunting, 72–73
  See also: Wolves
Dolphins, 29
Domestic animals, 77
Drones, 109
Dung, eating, 6–7

E
Eel, 91
Eggs, 46–47
Egotistical altruism, 110–111
Elephant seals, 44
Elephants, 6–7, 16–17, 114–115
  bull, 37
Environmental imprinting,
  23
Ethology, 4–15
  human, 14
  hypotheses, 6–7
  tools, 10
Evolution of behavior,
  26–35

F
Facial expressions, 104–105
Family, 106–107
Fear reaction, 37
Feeding:
  behavior, 37
  territories, 78
Females, 44–55
Filter feeders, 21
Fingers, bunched, 25
Fish, 94
  butterfly, 95
  cleaner, 94
  clown, 95
  deep sea angler, 20
  eel, 91
  jellyfish, 57
  labroides dimidiatus, 45
  salpa, 94
  seahorse, 63
  starfish, 20
  three-spined stickleback, 8
  viperfish, 71
Fly, 5
Fox, 78–79, 82
Fratricide, 60
Freshwater turtle, 26
Frilled dragon, 19
Fungus gardens, 97

G
Gametes, 46
Gazelles, 71
Gender, 44–55
  roles, 48–49, 54–55
Genetics, 30–31, 85
Gestures, 25
Giant panda, 118
Gnu, 72, 86–87
Great Crested Grebe, 50
Grooming, 102
Groups as protection, 69

H
Habitat, 78–93
Hamadryas, 100–101
Hares, 67
Heredity, 17–18
Hermaphrodites, 45
Hierarchies:
  reproductive, 100–101
  social, 107
Homing pigeons, 90
Hormones, role of, 38–40
Horsemen, 76
Humans, 76–77, 106–107
  altruism, 115–117
  behavior, 24–25
  body language, 24–25
  cycles, 41–43
  development, 64–65
  dispersion, 92–93
  ethology, 14
  family, 106–107
Humpback whale, 88–89
Hunters, 20
  communicating, 77
  lore, 12
Hunting, 71–77
Hypothesis, 5, 10

I
Imprinting, 21–23
Inborn behavior, 17–18
  humans, 24

Inbreeding, 85
Individual territory, 86
Information:
  effect of, 34–35
  gathering, 4
  processing, 5–6
Innate behavior, 17–18
Insects:
  ants, 104
  bees, 90, 108–109
  flies, 5
  ladybugs, 67
  societies, 96
  termites, 97
  walkingstick, 66
Instinct, 16–17
Interspecies altruism,
  118–119
Involution, 20

J
Jacana, 48–49
Jellyfish, 57

K
Kangaroo, 62

L
Labroides dimidiatus, 45
Lacerta viridis, 67
Ladakhi, 55
Ladybugs, 67
Language, 34
  body, 24–25
  facial expressions,
    104–105
Learned behavior, 17–18
  humans, 24
Learning, 21
  usefulness, 19
Lesser black-backed gulls,
  80
Limpkin, 48
Lion, 16
Lizard, 27

Lone wolf, 37
Lorenz, Konrad, 13–14
Lynx, 82

M
Macaques, 32–33
Magnetic field, 9
Males, 44–55
Marking, 10
Mechanisms of behaviors, 8–9
Memorization, 17, 21, 113
Mesonychids, 29
Migration, 39, 86–89
Mole rats, 110–111
Monogamy, 46, 50
Movement, 7
Muscle cells, 4
Musk oxen, 75
Mutations, 30
Mutual aid, 114–115

N
Natural selection, 31–32, 74, 77
Navigation, 90–91
Nerve cells, 4
Nesting, 11

O
Observation, 5–6
Offspring, 56–65
  caring for, 58
Olfactive imprinting, 23
Olfactory receptors, 5
Orientation, 90–91
Overcrowding, 40
Oysters, 20

P
Packs, 72
Pairing, 11, 15
Panda, giant, 118
Parenting, 56–65

Peacock, 52
Peacock worm, 21
Peahen, 53
Penguin, 63
Pigeons, 27, 90
Polyandry, 46
Polygamy, 46, 50, 54
Population density, 40
Porcupine, 67
Prairie dog, 68–69
Predators, 66–77
  facing, 16
  societies, 72
Predictions, 10
Prey, 66–77
Progeny, 60–61
Protective:
  coloring, 67
  strategies, 66–71

Q
Queen bees, 108–109

R
Rats, 18
  mole, 110–111
Reciprocal altruism, 116
Red fox, 78–79, 82
Reedbuck, 52–53
Reproduction, 39, 44–45
  offspring, care of, 58
  sexual, 45–46
  strategies, 56–57
Reproductive:
  caste, 96
  hierarchies, 100–101
Rhinoceros, 58
Rituals, 103
Robin, 82
Roles, 110–113

S
Salpa, 94
Scientific method, 6–7

Scorpion, 5
Sea turtles, 9, 91
Seahorse, 63
Seals, elephant, 44
Seasonal:
  behavior, 36–43
  cycles, 38
Selection:
  artificial, 30, 74
  natural, 31–32
  sexual, 52–54
Sense cells, 4–5
Senses, 4
Sexual:
  dimorphism, 50
  reproduction, 45–46
  selection, 52–54
Shells, 26
Sighting, 5
Signals, alarm, 69
Simple behavior, 20
Skunk, 66
Smiling, 25
Snails, 45
Social:
  behavior, 94–107
  cohesion, 106
  development, 76
  hierarchies, 107
  interaction, 14
  organization, 98
Societies:
  communication, 104–105
  insect, 96
  origin of, 42
  predators, 72
Soldiers, 96
Sperm, 46–47
Sperm whale, 56–57
Spiders, 18
Sports, 14
Stag, 82
Starfish, 20

T
Tags, 10
Technological culture, 35
Termite nest, 97
Territoriality, flexible, 86
Territory, 30, 78–93
  expansion, 78
  feeding, 78
Three-spined stickleback,
  8
Tinbergen, Niko, 13
Tom cats, 99
Tortoise, 27
Tribal culture, 35
Troops, 100–101
Turtle:

freshwater, 26
sea, 91

V
Verreaux eagles, 60
Veterinary medicine,
  119
Viperfish, 71
von Frisch, Karl, 13

W
Walkingstick, 66
Weaning, 72
Weapons, 72
Whales, 28–29
  humpback, 88–89

sperm, 56–57
  See also: Cetaceans
White stork, 38–39
Wintering, 39
Wolves, 17, 30, 102
  lone, 37
Woodpecker, 27
  finch, 19
Workers, 90, 96, 109

Y
Yanomami, 54
Yawning, 25

Z
Zebras, 16

Acknowledgments

The illustrations displayed in this volume are new and original. They have been realized upon a project by DoGi s.p.a. that owns its copyright.

ILLUSTRATIONS:
Archivio DoGi: 4b; Luciano Crovato and Gianni Mazzoleni: 19br; Luciano Crovato and Gianni Mazzoleni with the help of Ferruccio Cucchiarini: 59b; Gian Paolo Faleschini: 4tl, 26t, 38, 39t, 39br, 39c, 50–51, 58–59, 63l, 64–65, 68–69, 70–71, 74–75t, 80–81, 84–85, 94tl, 102–103, 104–105; Gian Paolo Faleschini with the help of Leonardo Meschini: 5, 6–7, 8–9, 10–11, 12–13, 14–15, 16–17, 18, 19t, 19bl, 21, 22–23, 26–27, 28–29, 30–31, 32–33, 36–37, 39bl, 40–41, 44–45, 46–47, 48–49, 56–57, 60–61, 63br, 74–75b, 78–79, 82–83, 88–89, 94–95, 100–101, 110–111, 112–113, 114–115, ; Inklink, Florence: 9tr, 14–15, 24–25, 34–35, 76–77, 106–107, 116–117; Inklink, Florence with the help of Antonella Pastorelli: 66tl, 66br, 90, 96–97, 104b, 108–109; Inklink, Florence with the help of Theo Caneschi: 56tl, 87; Alessandra Micheletti: 71t, 71c.

REPRODUCTIONS AND DOCUMENTS:
DoGi s.p.a. has done its best to dis-

cover possible rights of third parties. We apologize for any omissions or mistakes that might have occurred, and we will be pleased to introduce the appropriate corrections in the later editions of this book.
Archivio ACE: 66bl; Massimo Duccini Viareggio: 93c; Farabolafoto, Milan: 43b, 54; Farabolafoto, Milan/Overseas/ Dani-Jeske: 53t; Farabolafoto, Milan/ Overseas/Claudio Galasso: 67t; Farabolafoto, Milan/Overseas/Jacana: 90; Farabolafoto, Milan/Overseas/ Jacana/Varin Visage: 119; Farabolafoto, Milan/Overseas/Fabio Pedrazzi: 99b; Farabolafoto, Milan/Overseas/Renato Polo: 98; Farabolafoto, Milan/Overseas/ J. C. Revy: 53b, 55; Granata Stock: 93r; K&B, Florence/Giuliano Valsecchi: 45; The Image Bank, Rome/Guido Alberto Rossi: 92l; The Image Bank, Rome/ Harald Sund: 92r; Andrea Innocenti: 52b, 67b; International Colour Press, Milan/ Peter David: 20; Panda Photo, Rome/ M. Bonora: 91b; Panda Photo, Rome/ G. Cubitt: 81tr; Panda Photo, Rome/ Dia Contact/ A. Visage: 44; Panda Photo, Rome/N. J. Dennis: 81tl; Panda Photo, Rome/ FLPA/ M. Callan: 99t; SIE, Rome/The

Stock Market/Bob Abraham: 91t; SIE, Rome/The Stock Market/Tom Brakefield: 52t; SIE, Rome/The Stock Market/John Feingersh: 118; SIE, Rome/The Stock Market/Brian Peterson: 62; SIE, Rome/ The Stock Market/Kennan Ward: 102; SIE, Rome/The Stock Market/ Zefa/ Bach: 70; SIE, Rome/Zefa Minden Pictures/F. Lanting: 58, 63; SIE, Rome/Zefa Minden Pictures/ F. Nicklink: 105; The Stock Market: 42–43; The Stock Market/Dimitri Kessel: 86–87; The Stock Market/ H. Lloyd: 93l; The Stock Market/ Ariel Skelley: 92c.

COMPUTER ARTWORKS:
Sebastiano Ranchetti: 89, 92–93.

COVER: Gian Paolo Faleschini

FRONTISPIECE: Luciano Crovato and Gianni Mazzoleni with the collaboration of Ferruccio Cucchiarini tr; Gian Paolo Faleschini tl, b.

Abbreviations: t: top/b: bottom/ c: center/r: right/l: left